Thinking

ADRIAAN T. PEPERZAK

Thinking

From Solitude to Dialogue and Contemplation

Fordham University Press

New York 2006

I dedicate this report
to those of you who will
read the entire text

Copyright © 2006 by Fordham University Press

All rights reserved. No part of this publication may be reproduced, stored in a retrieval system, or transmitted in any form or by any means—electronic, mechanical, photocopy, recording, or any other—except for brief quotations in printed reviews, without the prior permission of the publisher.

Library of Congress Cataloging in Publication Data

Peperzak, Adriaan Theodoor, 1929–
   Thinking : from solitude to dialogue and contemplation / by Adriaan T. Peperzak.
      p.   cm.
   Includes bibliographical references and index.
   ISBN 0-8232-2618-2 (cloth : alk. paper) — ISBN 0-8232-2619-0 (pbk. : alk. paper)
   1. Thought and thinking—Philosophy.   2. Communication—Philosophy.   3. Prayer—Christianity.   4. Philosophical theology.   I. Title.
   B105.T54P47 2006
   190—dc22
2006002696

Printed in the United States of America
08 07 06   5 4 3 2 1
First edition

CONTENTS

Preface   vii
Introduction   xi

1. I Think   1
   The Self-Conception of Modern Philosophy 1 *The Practice of Modern Philosophy*
   6 *The Philosophical Republic* 18 *From "I Think" to "We Speak"* 22

2. Speaking   25
   Speaking To/Speaking About 25 *You Speak to Me* 29 *Responding* 31 *Teacher and
   Pupil* 37 *Listening Is Learning* 41 *Dialogue* 45 *From Dialogue to Conversation*
   50 *Hermeneutics and/or Conversation?* 54

3. Philosophy as Conversation   56
   Sharing and Originality 56 *Issues* 58 *The Thinker* 60 *Individual Thinkers and
   the Good* 67 *The Community of Difference* 69 *You and I Are Speaking* 74
   Speaking and Writing 76 *From Listening to Speaking in Philosophy* 78 *Dialogue*
   87 *Singularization of the Truth* 90 *You* 93 *The Audience* 97 *Proximity and
   Distance* 103 *You and I* 105 *Dear Reader* 109 *System and Dialogue* 112
   Conversation and Universality 115 *Philosophy and Wisdom* 118 *Truth and
   Conversation* 122 *Participation* 124 *Contemplation or Colloquium* 125

4. From Thinking to Prayer   127
   Philosophy and Theology 127 *The Republic of Philosophy* 135 *Being Christian and
   Philosopher* 136 *Free Thinking as a Right* 137 *Faith versus Survey* 140 *Faith and*

Adoration 142 *Trust—Gratitude—Hope* 145 *Love* 148 *A Faithful Life* 151 *Communion* 153 *Answering the Word* 154 *Prayer and Theology* 156 *The Universe (Cosmotheology)* 157 *Distance and Intimacy* 158 *Faith and Dialogue* 161

Notes   165

PREFACE

Philosophy entails thinking. And thinking entails living a human life. Philosophy also entails thinking about thinking—and about the lives from which philosophies emerge.

For more than a century, numerous philosophers have drawn our attention to the dependence of philosophy on common facts and events that cannot be constructed or reconstructed, and even less destructed, by thinking alone. Such facts are, for example, the individual thinker's unique birth and education, the tradition(s) and the ethos of the surrounding society with its particular culture and history, the language used, and the religion (with or without God) in which each thinker is rooted. However, one basic, decisive, and irreducible fact has not received sufficient attention: as emerging from a lived life, thinking, including thinking about thinking, entails speaking.

Philosophers speak—or, rather, philosophers listen to a speaking that is already there and then respond to it, thus becoming speakers in turn. All speaking is imitation and response: handing on what we have heard, but transforming it through appropriation and donation.

This book focuses on the speaking aspect of philosophical thought. It invites you, Reader, to listen and look into the to and fro that structures philosophy as a peculiar kind of communication. The central issue can be evoked through the word *addressing*: what distinguishes speech (or writing) from rumination is its being directed or addressed by someone to someone. A text, for example, is nothing, if it is not directed, addressed, dedicated, proposed, sent, or delivered to someone, who, as recipient, is different from the writer. To be involved in philosophy is being part of a history of messages and responses through which thinkers offer their thoughts to listeners as invitations to use them for new messages. As a history of proposals and propositions, the practice of philosophy is an ongoing tradition of responsive renewals without end—thanks to many turns and returns in speaking.

After a critical sketch in chapter 1 of the methodological paradigm that is characteristic for the self-conception of modern philosophy, the second chapter presents a succinct analysis of speaking, which the third chapter transposes to the level of philosophy as dialogical history. In chapter 4, the question is asked of whether philosophy also must be understood as a form of listening and responding to words of God.

In all chapters, the distinction between speaking (and thinking) *about* and speaking *to* (and thinking toward) is considered to be decisive for the practice and the definition of human life and the role of thinking in it. If you press me to summarize these considerations in a thesis, I would answer the following.

Philosophical speech or writing *about* neither honors nor reveals the full truth of human persons (you, him, her, us, all of you, them, and me), but it is necessary. We must redeem its irreverence by subordinating it, as a component, to a form of addressing (proposing, offering, dedication) that respects the addressee as an "end in itself."

Thinking and speaking about God is even more deficient, but it is not less necessary. Meditation about the archaic Word cannot reach the Speaker unless it turns into prayer, or—as Descartes wrote—into a contemplation that makes me "consider, admire, and adore the beauty of God's immense light, as much as the eyesight of my blinded mind can tolerate."

* * *

Several friends, many more than I can mention here, have assisted me in the writing of this book; I am profoundly grateful to all of them. Allow me to name and thank here particularly those who co-operated most closely in the process: my wife Angela, who encouraged me to write these pages; Jason Barret and Mark McCreary, who checked and corrected my English; Marjolein Oele and Joe Linn, who took care of the computerized version; Jean Tan, who helped me in composing the index; and Mary Christian, who edited the final text.

Chicago—Wilmette
July 3, 2005

INTRODUCTION

If "thinking" could be accepted as a name for philosophy, a successful phenomenology of thinking would be a part of metaphilosophy. Instead of "metaphilosophy" we can use the expression "philosophy of philosophy," but we should not suggest from the outset that the phenomenon of "philosophical thought" can be fully understood from a philosophical perspective alone. If philosophy were the highest level of thought, then such an assumption would be obvious. However, we would be too hasty if, without thorough investigation, we excluded the possibility of a still higher, deeper, more original, or more encompassing perspective or dimension.

Before answering the question of philosophy's height, depth, and competence, we must know how philosophizing is done. How do philosophers think? How do their thoughts emerge from the life they live and the philosophical, literary, scientific, religious, or theological traditions with which they have become familiar? What and how do they borrow from their predecessors? How do they converse with one another, teach their pupils, influence their audiences, develop and update their skills? How do some of them inaugurate revolutions, while others make themselves useful as teachers, interpreters, or editors?

The task that lies before us implies so many observations and analyses, including historical, psychological, and sociological ones, that any attempt at accomplishing it can hardly be more than a partial—and therefore selective and somewhat biased—contribution. In trying to offer such a contribution, I am aware of my own limitations, but these should not withhold me from proposing a tentative and provisional approach. In particular, I will insist on a few points that, for many years, have struck me as relevant for a rethinking of the metaphilosophical project, although they are often neglected.

After a quick characterization of the typical presentation that hails modern philosophy as a combination of self-conscious experience and autonomous thought according to a self-guaranteed logic, I will confront this presentation with the practice in which philosophers since Parmenides and Heraclitus have been involved: a practice in which heteronomous elements, such as beliefs, faiths, desires, as well as education, discussion, and other forms of communication, have played a much larger role than most modern theories of thought suggest or permit. One of the "elements" of this practice that is often forgotten is the speaking through which philosophers address their questions and answers to one another. However, study of this element demands a phenomenology—at least an embryonic one—of speaking in general. If speaking implies urging interlocutors to answer what has been addressed to them, the dialogical structure of philosophy is also revealed to be necessary and essential for all thought. Besides the difficult—and to a certain extent novel—questions that emerge from the dialogical reciprocity of philosophical speaking, that which is spoken about—the "content" or the "said"—must also be studied, not only for the reasons forwarded by all treatises of metaphilosophy, but also because it binds speakers and listeners together in a shared concentration. One of the questions that arise from the ongoing conversation about issues that gather the participants into a community of thinkers is the question of their interest in those issues. The philosophical eros that animates the interlocutors must therefore be interpreted in light of the Desire that inspires their lives.[1] Since the search for the desideratum to which this desire points is decisive for the meaning of a human life, philosophy can ignore neither the ultimate attraction that seems to surpass all other desiderata, nor the other kinds of quests for the most beloved, especially in religion and art. Consequently, the relation between philosophy and other erotic pursuits, such as morality, love, art, faith, theology, and contemplation, must be rethought and redefined. A complete philosophy of philosophy would thus imply a philosophy of the entire culture. Here, however, I will restrict my meditations to the connections between thinking, speaking, and adoration. Does philosophy restrict itself to finite issues or does it deserve an absolute commitment, in competition with religious faiths and other basic convictions?

ONE

I Think

The Self-Conception of Modern Philosophy

For a long time, philosophy has presented itself as a fundamental form of thinking based on experience and logic. Besides fundamentality or originariness, its characteristics most emphasized were universality and autonomy.

Modern Western philosophy owes its origin to a rebellion against religious and theological dominance.[1] It wanted to free itself from all authorities except the undeniable authority of self-observed givenness and demonstrative thought. All opinions and beliefs, including the real or putative wisdoms of ancient and recent "fathers" and "mothers," should be ignored in philosophy, even if they continue to inform the practice of most lives. From now on, thinkers should take the entire responsibility for true and self-certain wisdom—including the technical, medical, moral, political, and religious knowledge on which an emancipated praxis had to be based. Since complete ignorance with regard to traditional wisdom is impossible (it would reduce a person to a clumsy monkey), the boundary between tradition and a new beginning was construed as a separation between two lives: while the thinkers' social and personal lives continued to be determined by historical circumstances, traditional customs, and personal adventures, their philosophical development was ruled by abstract certainties in isolation from as yet unjustified practices and opinions.[2] The real but naïve and philosophically spurious praxis from which modern thinkers take their departure changes, as part of their reflection, into a new, philosophically more justified dimension of life. On the way to a complete justification, one must avoid all non-philosophical interference, in order to progressively ascertain a completely valid version of one's entire life. The project of a newly conceived, philosophically justified life must develop into a mature, no longer naïve and uncertain but empirically and rationally well-formed life that would replace the insufficiently examined praxis from which it springs. If philosophy could accomplish this task, the modern dream of becoming one's own father and mother—a human kind of *causa sui*, at least in thought—would no longer be a mere fiction.

By isolating the thinker's theory not only from the ruling opinions and customs, but also from his own praxis, modern thought breaks its prephilosophical ties with the communities, traditions, stories, and histories in which that praxis—the thinker's own concrete life—is engaged. Thinking is a strictly individual affair: *cogitare* needs an "I" to come alive. The new homunculus of modernity is named *Ego cogito*. Instead of a church, a culture, or a République des Lettres, the subject of thought is an individual "I" that thinks and rethinks all that must be thought.

This "I," however, is manifold. Indeed, as long as the thinker remembers that he has taken over the responsibility for universal wisdom from the old religions and traditions, his ego thinks and speaks in the name of all egos. Instead of serving a Church or State or Culture, the philosopher has become a functionary of Humanity. Later, when individual thinkers will have agreed on their conclusions, a new philosophically legitimate community will be established on the basis of universally valid truth. As long as individuals are still focused on isolated attempts at discovery, helped by one another only through mutual exchange and testing of their demonstrations, we must believe and prove that all egos have access through thinking to the universally valid and recognizable truth.

Being responsible for the universal truth, the I-who-thinks is eager to experience all that is given outside and inside the philosophical (i.e., abstract, simultaneously isolated and universal) ego. Its experiences must be real, neither fictive nor transformed by the imagination of poetically gifted or "speculative" observers. Empirical givenness should be pure, uncontaminated by "subjective" confusions and biases. Experience, though necessarily self-conscious, must be "objective," potentially universal, neutral, and—above all—impersonal.

Several classics of modern thought have identified pure experience with mathematically or physically stylized patterns of given reality. By doing so, they narrowed the horizons of their observation and blinded themselves to many phenomena and aspects of the universe. After more than a century of phenomenology, it is no longer necessary to dwell on the fundamental mistakes that were made by identifying objective reality with experiences that fit Descartes's or Locke's framework of "clear and distinct ideas," but it is still very difficult to agree on the limits and the validity of experiential evidence.

Taking the phenomenological critique of the modern practice and theory of experience for granted,[3] I will at this moment not insist on the various ways in which the entire wealth of phenomena exists and shows itself, but instead focus on the universality that the modern *cogito* claims for both its experiences and its logical principles.

That modern philosophy continues to view the universe as an all-encompassing but grounded universe is what links it to the oldest traditions of philosophy. All the modern classics from Hobbes to

Hegel focus on the totality of beings and ask how it can exist in the way it does. What seems new, however, is the assumption that "I" (the abstractly isolated ego), by means of radical abstractions, can isolate universally evident data and principles out of which I can reconstruct the real world in which we always already have been living. We want to understand the whole of all things by rebuilding, as conceptual designers, the universe on the basis of undeniable material and self-evident principles. The possibility of such reconstruction (including the abstract and the real egos by which it is supported) is a necessary postulate of the modern project, if it wants to maintain both its autonomy and its universal responsibility toward all egos. Though it is true that this responsibility has not been overly emphasized by the modern classics, the fact that they publicly proclaimed their thoughts as universally valid implied a belief that they were serving humanity as a whole. Another debatable postulate implied in their basic assumptions is that the language in which they expressed their thought could be translated into other languages without losing the universal truth conveyed by it.

The modern project thus determined philosophy as a solitary but socially responsible task for hermits who remained dedicated to humanity. That only a few thinkers succeeded in somewhat accomplishing this task is understandable. They deserve the liturgies we regularly celebrate in their honor, but the proliferation of substantially different theories, issued from the modern project, gives us pause to question the very project. How is it possible that the modern agreement caused such remarkable differences between the systems that were generated in the pursuit of its clear and distinct guidelines? And, on the other hand, how can we explain the striking similarities that connect the modern theories not only with one another, but also with the ancient and medieval philosophies that were loudly condemned by the modern revolution?

In the heyday of the Enlightenment,[4] the enthusiasm for modernity expressed itself in an almost eschatological expectation of endless advancement and progress. True, Hegel understood that the history of thought followed a more complicated course, but he too maintained the progressive pattern, though dialectically varied, to explain the history of European philosophy and civilization in general as driven by an inner logic toward total comprehension. Other simplistic patterns have been employed to make sense of the philosophical pluralism that characterizes all the epochs of Western history, including the modern epoch, whose explicit purpose lay in the overcoming of that pluralism by the conquest of universal certainty about demonstrated truth. Post-Hegelians such as Marx, Nietzsche, and Heidegger have criticized the soundness of the modern project, but even their views of universality, autonomy, progress, and history bear the marks of modernity.

If the pluralism of philosophy, instead of being overcome by a methodic realization of the modern principles, has exacerbated the conflict between styles, chapels, schools, and traditions, could the cause of this conflict lie in the project itself or its assumptions? The autonomy of pure reason has failed to yield more agreement among philosophers than their past adherence to a single religion. The modern appreciation of universality as a distinctive feature of the truth has been destroyed in an almost universal war among stars and epigones. On the other hand, however, a certain affinity among contemporary philosophers cannot be altogether denied. Is perhaps affinity-in-difference a more faithful realization of human universality than the rigid universality of a theoretical unisono brought about by mere instantiations of the genus rationality? Does the modern conception of *ego cogito* imply a denial of the radical and original difference that belongs to all concrete individualizations of universality? Perhaps another concept or quasi-concept of universality is more authentic, faithful, promising, and true than the schizophrenic universality that divided the modern individual into a concrete practice of one's own and an abstract generality representative of being human as such.

The Practice of Modern Philosophy

Did the philosophical heroes of the last five centuries practice the laws of modern orthodoxy? The following answer will focus on three aspects of their practice: (1) its relation to the proclaimed autonomy, (2) the (relative) solitude of the modern thinkers and the monological character of their thoughts, and (3) the philosophical "republic" that emerged from the modern practice.

HERMENEUTICS Historical studies of modern philosophies from Hobbes to Heidegger have shown how modern thinkers have borrowed many convictions and thoughts from premodern traditions without proving the legitimacy of these assumptions. Apparently, the moderns did not quite succeed in keeping their philosophical ego separate from the cultural customs in which they were educated. Sometimes they were not even aware of their own naïve use of some traditional views that later would be unmasked as far from self-evident; on other occasions they tried to prove certain suppositions without success. When we, with the greatest benevolence and perspicacity, try to reconstruct the theories of the main philosophers from Hobbes and Descartes to Heidegger and Levinas, we invariably run up against the impossibility of demonstrating that all the parts, and especially some basic ones, of any of those theories satisfy the requirement of necessarily following from self-evident experience in combination with self-evident logical and epistemological principles. The stubborn pursuit of an ideal autonomy—necessary presupposition of every fully independent philosophy—has not led to a rigorously demonstrated science whose validity justifies its claim to be the truth for all humanity. On the contrary, five centuries of thorough thought seem rather to have resulted in general discouragement and despair with regard to the original purpose.

In contrast to those who faithfully continue to work within the boundaries of the modern framework, albeit with greater modesty, many others, who also claim to be philosophers, have given up certain axioms of modernity. Among these, the axiom of philosophy's complete autonomy has become questionable. Many authors have pointed out how much philosophy has always depended on situational and historical factors; on religious, literary, political, economic, psychological, and moral conditions; and on philosophical traditions that preceded and survived the birth of any new beginning, even the most revolutionary of all. Each philosophy can be seen as the typical expression of a spiritual family, a historical epoch, a cultural climate; its fundamental assumptions express a super-personal mentality (a "spirit") equally recognizable in artistic, religious, economic, and political epochs and developments. After concretizing itself in characteristically Greek and Latin philosophies, thought has developed into French, German, English, Dutch, Italian, Spanish, and other branches and discovered that it cannot maintain a strict separation between its claims to universality and the language it speaks.

Twentieth-century hermeneutics has developed a metaphilosophical perspective from which all philosophies are seen as delayed attempts to express and partially justify a variety of positions that emerge from a particular time and culture. Each philosophy seems to be rooted in a specific soil and made up of a complex combination of geographic, epochal, linguistic, and spiritual elements that cannot be completely justified by the thought in which they are integrated. To what extent belief or faith or some kind of fundamental trust play decisive roles among these elements is a question that, for obvious reasons, is stubbornly avoided by many participants in the philosophical enterprise. The question is decisive, however, because it bears directly on the question of the (whole or partial) autonomy of thought.

EGOLOGY AND SOLITUDE Since *Selbstdenken*—thinking on one's own—was the device of the modern emancipation,[5] all that was proposed as true had to be verified by each thinking individual who was confronted with it. Every thinker was fully responsible for all judgments about truth and falsehood, certainty and uncertainty, clarity and vagueness or obscurity, and so on.

To be judge and controller of all truth, freedom and universal validity are essential. Modern philosophers have defined freedom as self-determination: I determine whatever I think, choose, decide, pursue, and do. Another name for it is "free will": the will as freely—i.e., willingly—willing. Not only do I will all the actions, words, and expressions that issue from me as a rational subject, but I also will the very will that is expressed in all of them. I will my will as origin and master of its own willing.[6] As "master and possessor" not only of the world but also of my will, I appropriate the universe in order to discover and use and transform its elements and energies for the benefit of humanity. This appropriation cannot stop at nature; it inevitably extends its mastery to the social facts and rules of politics, economics, and psychology; it will even redesign and engineer the laws of aging and procreation.

Our culture seems to be obsessed with the ideal of a humanity that generates, possesses, and guarantees its own existence. That the concept of such a *causa sui* is self-contradictory does not impede us from compromising with an approximation of this fantasy. A shadow of it is pursued when a philosophical ego (re)constructs in thought alone the universe whose existence is due to other-than-human powers.

From Descartes to Hegel, the modern classics continued to believe in a radical difference between the cause of the universe and the human will, but in philosophy the overall design could and should be recreated theoretically. The ultimate horizon of human life still was God's infinity in its transcendence beyond the finite cosmos of human existence. Though Kant restricted rigorous knowledge to the finite universe while restricting access to God to the necessary implications of a morally and rationally justified belief, Fichte, Schelling, and Hegel could not quite suppress their desire to reintroduce God into the heart of philosophical theory. From Feuerbach on, many philosophers have declared or implied that "God" either was a mask for something more finite (e.g., Humanity or History), or was deceased—at least in philosophy. The question of how the universe could exist was ignored, ridiculed, or declared a false question, while only a few thinkers seemed to notice that everything—not only in philosophy—had profoundly changed since the infinite horizon of the tradition was swept away and replaced by the terribly narrow framework of a finite world.

The modern ego thought itself capable of reconstructing at least the finite universe. Geometrical analysis and synthesis had provided the paradigm of such a de- and reconstruction in a particular dimension. Philosophy had to do the same for the overall dimension of the human cosmos and its various levels. The *cogito* would be the workplace where the universal system of all things (including the living and the thinking ego) was received in order to be disassembled and rebuilt. The all-encompassing reality should fit within the confines of an (abstract, isolated) thinking ego. Emerging in ego's consciousness through the universalization of its individual, extremely limited experience, the universe should be reproduced conceptually through the rational justification of its factual essence and existence. "I" alone, the lonely thinker, who am at the same time this individual and the universal paradigm of all individuals, am the (re)builder and justifier of the world—in theory, my (universally valid and therefore everyone's) theory.

Even when German Idealism or Husserl realized that the Ego of such a *cogito* could not be identified with a human individual in isolation from God, history, or humanity, the "transcendental ego" to which they appealed remained accessible to thinking individuals. Though I (for example, Descartes, Kant, or Hegel) am not "the I," I still can tell you what and how "the I" (who is neither you, nor I, but rather a consciousness "above" or "behind" or "deep within" you and me) thinks. Abandoning this assumption would destroy our conviction that we think in the name and at the service of humanity.

Against the one-sided emphasis on a transcendental—and therefore universal—consciousness from Descartes to Husserl, many post-Hegelian historians, sociologists, psychologists, anthropologists, linguists, and psychoanalysts have attacked the myth of philosophy's autonomy. We can no longer maintain a clear-cut separation between the self-thinking ego and concretely lived individuality. Each thinker is—also in his thinking—as much the product of traditions, teachers, educators, communities, events, and so on, as a source of unique and more or less original thoughts. Thinking, like life in general, is preceded and (co)-determined by many influences and authorities that it cannot reduce to universally indubitable facts or proofs. Good thought presupposes reading and training; like religion and poetry or art in general, philosophy, too, retrieves existing patterns and borrows from the heroes of its history. Without taking for granted at least some of the presuppositions—the *doxai*—that are generally accepted in the culture of one's spiritual family, it is not possible to say anything at all, and the hope that I, at some point, will be able to demonstrate the truth of my point of departure (including its method and all of its assumptions) is never fulfilled. Phenomenology has made us aware of the impossibility of capturing all the data and phenomena that should be experienced and of understanding them as necessary components of the existing universe. Most appearances and experiences, especially the interesting and important ones, are too ambiguous, too codetermined by the circumstances and horizons in which they are caught, to allow for a fundamental orthodoxy. Not only being as such, but dogs, stars, flowers, mountains, and especially human individuals demand that we deal with them with the most attentive and appropriate sensibility before we venture to say anything about their givenness as such. Of all phenomena it is true that they *are* and must be said "*pollachōs*."[7] None of them can be cut off from the historical world of concrete thinkers, whose lives can never coincide with the development of their abstract or transcendental *cogito*s. If we still want to maintain a distinction between their philosophical (self-)consciousness and their worldly, individual, historical life—and there are good reasons for doing so[8]—the Cartesian separation and its theoretical foundation must be transformed into another relationship between thinking and living. Culture, nation, language, tradition, historical developments, and individual growth participate in the genealogy of a philosophical work, which cannot expel all of them once it has crystallized into a settled form. The ladders cannot be thrown away. One can try not to settle in order to remain mobile and in flux, but death is inexorable when an adventure is transformed into an oeuvre: nobody else can relive the movement that stopped when the thinker was buried under a monument. What we can make of the dead person's path is a simplified (re)construction of its orientation, method, stages, and—answered or unanswered—questions that arose on the way. Such a (re)construction is an invitation to see whether it offers possibilities to other philosophers, who perhaps can use it in their attempts to *re*think the issues for themselves (i.e., as their own thoughts, arising from combined sources) in order to illuminate human life from other angles.

MONOLOGY   Concentration on interesting issues cannot confine itself to fragments of the historical world in which the thinker participates. Since thinking connects and grounds, its subject matter is "all things" or the universe, while its questions are motivated by a "why?" that constantly reemerges as long as it has not discovered a first or original "therefore": a "beginning" or *arche* of all *archai*. Philosophy cannot help wanting to be principled ("archaic") and universal. *Cogito* means: I want and must think the whole in light of its "first beginning" or "principle" (its *arche* or *principium*, which is also the ultimate, because the *arche* and the *telos* are the same). Philosophy's subject matter and method thus follow from the modern project of thought. All its dimensions refer to the "first" and "last" or the "beginning" and the "end" of the *omnitudo realitatis*.[9] Its breadth embraces all beings, its depth refers to the most fundamental of all supports, its length stretches out over all times and eternity, and its height points to something that transcends all heights (and therefore also all other dimensions and the very dimensionality of all finite beings as components of the universe.

"I think" means that "I" (the isolated and abstract ego) find myself confronted with the allness that encompasses everything, including myself. In Descartes's description of this fact not only my own consciousness but also the idea of God was included. "I" still was conscious of God's presence to "me" as mediated through an idea: "the idea of the infinite."[10] However, this awareness dwindled away during the later development of philosophy, though Spinoza, Leibniz, Kant, and Hegel continued to affirm that the idea of God was the beginning and end of all serious thought. They thus integrated the framework that Augustine formulated in one of his youthful writings:

> *Augustine:* What I want to know is God and the soul.
> *Reason:* Nothing else?
> *Augustine:* Absolutely nothing.[11]

It is improbable that Augustine sought to exclude the cosmos, human society, and history from his relationship to God—the fact that he published his soliloquy with Reason expresses a less private interest—but it is certain that the modern classics included them in their framework, even if some deemed it necessary to first demonstrate that they existed. Even so, their allness (*omnitudo*) was from the beginning "seen" as originating from and illuminated by the infinite power of the Creator.

Everyone who publishes a philosophical text presupposes the existence of others who are able to follow its argument and—at least to a certain extent—to rethink what it tries to transmit. But to what extent are other humans included among the main issues a leading thinker must think? Modern philosophers wrote many texts about social facts and structures; intersubjective and political questions, however, rarely represented their main interest. Together with ethics, social and political questions were often delayed as secondary with regard to epistemological and metaphysical ones. First, the *Cogito* had to be developed into an overall conception of the universe. In doing this, *Ego* did not listen to or consult with others: the universal doubt had done away with all authorities; no new or old authorities should be brought in again. Insofar as thinkers expressed themselves in writing, they presupposed that other egos were reading, but insofar as their (self-)consciousness had not yet deduced other persons' or their own language, such listening and their own speaking were unreal and unwarranted. *Ego cogito* meant therefore the authorial ego that was alone with the universe, whatever, "besides" God and "me," this might contain.

The thinkers' solicitude expresses itself in (1) a specific kind of allness, and (2) a specific treatment of the universe. As long as their practice is motivated by the desire to "master and possess" the world,[12] their theoretical approach prefers *treatises* over other modes of approaching the truth. Instead of writing Platonic dialogues or participating in medieval disputations, I pursue my ideal—a panoramic and fully founded re-creation of the universe—in accordance with the purely rational and empirically warranted method of a solitary (but transcendentally regulated) thought. If I succeed, the result will be a systematic monologue—an overall System—that represents the universe. Through observation, abstraction, analysis, deduction, and reduction, synthesis, and (re)composition, my initial *cogito* has transformed the world into a systematic whole, while transforming itself into a conceptually clarified and amended version of the naïve consciousness from which I started. The treatise in which I summarize my silent discoveries is then offered for inspection to others who are supposed to share with me a universal reason and an equal capacity for experience.

Objections can be answered or accepted as reasons for amending my theory, but the idea that inventive and truthful thinking must lead to a universally valid system cannot be abandoned. In the end, ultimately, eschatologically, the truth must be recognized and accepted universally in the form of one coherent doctrine. Discussions are useful on the way to truth, but the truth itself can be found only in a final monologue, which then ought to be shared by all thinkers, even if these express their identical thoughts in a variety of languages.

The idea of a uniform system goes very well with a notion of reality according to which being is objectivity. If existence is seen as primarily objective, displaying itself panoramically before a reflective onlooker, it is relatively easy to produce a systematic blueprint of such a reality. Like Spinoza or Hegel, one can even try to capture the dynamic patterns that prevent us from reducing the totality of beings to a static architecture. As long as one adheres to the monological character of thought, however, differences between thinkers cannot have a significance other than that of provisional obstacles on the way to the one and total truth we must share. Dialogues are only didactical means to initiate or convert the ignorant, or else indications of unfinished business and ongoing divergence among the searchers.

The solitary character of modern philosophy is revealed in the rituals that the republic of thinkers has adopted for its commerce with philosophy and one another. Their writings are original, although they continue to paraphrase (explicitly, implicitly, or unwittingly) other thinkers who once were explicitly recognized as authorities. If they themselves are successful, they will be referred to as the heroes of modernity. Thus, the history of modern philosophy is often summed up by enumerating the names of Descartes, Hobbes, Spinoza, Leibniz, Locke, Hume, Kant, Fichte, Hegel, and Schelling. They are recognized as the new authorities because they seem to have realized the modern project better than others.

It is not surprising that some individuals excelled in producing what that project wanted all thinkers to produce. Not everyone is able to maintain the methodical separation between the abstract, transcendental ego that thinks and the concrete ego that lives. Some are more suited than others to the modern model of observation and experience, more perspicacious and inventive or more lucky in the modern sense of these words. The most gifted and intensely focused individuals have a chance to become stars or even suns in the realm of thought. They will be celebrated as leaders whose proximity must be sought—even if one might want to test the degree of one's own originality by challenging them. Though, in principle, every individual, thanks to the universality of reason, is able to evaluate the systems that are offered by the great thinkers, their authority seems to surpass the question of their verifiable correctness. Do they possess a secret that is not or cannot be revealed to lesser minds? How do we recognize their greatness? Can "greatness" in thought be explained in terms of the modern standards of logic and experience?

It is remarkable that the modern classics have acquired such authority in light of the fact that almost everyone who seriously evaluates their doctrines finds unexplained gaps or less-than-obvious intuitions in them. Were the demands of the modern project too difficult for human intellects, even the most powerful?

Whatever the answer may be, the model of the great solitary thinker has not been abandoned. Even during the epoch that—perhaps falsely—is called "postmodern," great names play a role that exceeds the quality of their demonstrations. Their works remain the models that are emulated by less established philosophers. When these come together in their conferences, they compete by individually presenting the result of their solitary preparations. The most ambitious among them try to rethink the fundamental assumptions of the general orthodoxy; others, who operate within this orthodoxy, revise or apply some of its issues. A period of questions and answers opens the possibility of a discussion, but rarely does the exchange transcend the level of unilateral clarification, unresolved contradiction, or friendly confirmation. With regard to the motivation for giving talks and papers, one can perhaps argue that the modern conception of philosophy favors career-oriented competition and private profit won by individual brilliance rather than a common concern for truth, despite the fact that universal truth motivated the rules and conditions of the modern method. The main question, however, concerns the objective and structural character of the "business" that has developed in the course of philosophy's modern history. If, for example, dialogue and conversation were seen as a better preparation for truth than a series of monologues, our conferences would take the form (not only the name) of colloquia or symposia. If contemplation and ascetic practices were believed to offer more lucid access to the mystery of truth, conferences would have to be prepared by renewals of the monastic tradition. We, however, invite one individual after another to read their monologues. Are we at all concerned about integration? Do we strive for the same purpose? What is our purpose, if it is not the all-embracing truth?

The individualization of thinking is obvious in the histories of philosophy written during the last five centuries. Taking the modern conception of autonomous thought for granted, even the interpretations of premodern philosophers were pressed into this model. Ancient heroes of thought were invited to the modern competition where they were sometimes praised but most often criticized and corrected, while medieval philosophers were generally distrusted and often discarded because of their allegiance to the Christian faith, which supposedly made their thought heteronomous. Having transformed all premodern philosophies into singular systems, a modern historian had to explain whether the multitude of historical systems, made simultaneous by a panoramic overview, offered an answer to the questions of the modern project. Were they loyal to the orthodox method? To what extent did they fulfill the decisive condition of autonomy in thinking and experience? Can they be amended and used as fragments of a truly enlightened system, which only now has become possible?

Most modern histories of philosophy interpret the chronological succession of systems as an ongoing progress in truth. If we believe them, philosophy has developed from a naïve and primitive beginning to a more complex and better demonstrated system. The positive findings of the past have been integrated, whereas the errors have been left behind. Progress dominated prior thinking thanks to some great individuals who absorbed all previously discovered truth in their works; progress will also lead the geniuses of today and the future.

Of course, the schema of a continuous progress is too simple, but on the whole—with intermezzi of decadence and ignorance—the advancement from Thales to modern Enlightenment is still maintained by most overviews. Hegel's monumental systemization of history as one ongoing unfolding of a simple but implicit beginning—interrupted by ten centuries of "dark Middle Ages"—has remained the model for subsequent historiographers of philosophy.

But how can this type of history be seen as a symptom of modern individualism? Did Hegel not reduce the individual thinkers to the role of mere voices through which the one and only supra-individual Spirit expresses itself in the various stages of its (self-)development? Yes, but (1) these expressions take the form of singular systems entitled "Plato," "Aristotle," "Kant," "Fichte," and so on, and (2) the Spirit itself is a (super-)Ego, which, notwithstanding the deficiency and incompleteness of its expressions, in the end will produce the whole and perfect truth in the form of one grandiose synthesis that can be fathomed by human individualities.

In contrast to the enlightened portrayal of philosophy's history, the climate of the post-Hegelian period has favored an emphasis on decadent and perverse developments. Some have even suggested that the course from Parmenides to twentieth-century philosophy represents one long descent. However, historical precision is not the greatest strength of all such global and necessarily simplistic schematizations. Before indulging in one of their varieties, we should try to become more familiar with the facts and more suspicious about the philosophical assumptions of any history of philosophy than even Hegel and Heidegger were.

If we can show that any history of philosophy is governed by a specific conception of philosophy's practice and theory, this could give us the distance necessary to put each specific history and its underlying philosophy in place, thus opening a space for other philosophies and histories. With regard to the standard history of philosophy, it is time to free all pre- and postmodern modes and contents of thought from the framework imposed on them by the modern epoch (and its reversals). Ancient Greek and medieval thought, for example, require an appropriate, in many ways un- or trans-modern and an un- or trans-scientific approach to reveal their repressed splendor. Despite its important—and not merely technological—discoveries, modernity has made us *also* poorer in experience and in thought.[13]

The Philosophical Republic

In mentioning philosophical rituals and "liturgies" above, we leapt over the question of whether modern philosophers, despite their radical individualism, still form a community.

ASSOCIATION   If it is true that every thinker is autonomous and fully responsible for the argumentation and the results of his or her thinking, is a community of thinkers then possible at all? The only union seems to consist in the sharing of universal Reason, which inhabits and rules their minds. Everyone is focused on the acquisition of the same truth, while the accepted method prescribes that one should not listen to any other authority or command than only reason itself and to one's own experience. Reason is our own, but at the same time, it is universal. We share rationality (without diminishing our personal shares in it) and this makes us human. As individuals, we are more human (and thus more ourselves) the more our thinking becomes universal. The regulation of my responsibility for the truth is not imposed on me by any master of wisdom, but by the demand of universality that characterizes my own consciousness. Individual self-regulation is my duty, while my rights and my solidarity with others are fully realized only when I remain loyal to the rational necessity that must be recognized by anyone who thinks. An exclusively individual philosophy is not possible, because the truth it discovers unites all who see its validity. However, modern universality demands that each individual consciousness (re)discovers the universal and unifying truth on its own. Vocation is either an extra-philosophical concept or an illusion.

If the only link connecting modern thinkers is the reason they share, then the realization of reason's demands in theory and practice is confided to autonomous individuals. This task is enormous. It cannot be accomplished in one lifetime, but demands cooperation, fellowship, and tradition. Discoveries and methodical procedures should be passed on in education, while cooperation implies consultation and discussion. An organization of common activities is necessary, and this demands institutions. But how do institutions emerge from individualistic thinkers? Their belonging together cannot precede their choice because, if that were the case, it would rob them of their sovereignty. The only way in which an alliance of modern thinkers is possible lies in the shared decision of those who, recognizing the necessity of cooperation, choose to associate with one another. A modern community of autonomous thinkers must be based on a contract among freely consenting individuals. Such a contract is imagined as the effect of many individual decisions that, by some fortunate event, coincide in their willing of the same. It is not difficult to develop this argument into a theory about the essentially "free" and "democratic" character of modern philosophy. Whether the practice adequately expresses this theory is another question; the theoretical coherence between contractualism and autonomy seems duly guaranteed. If Hegel objects that a free association is not yet a community and that the latter demands a non-chosen—and in this sense *a priori*—principle of cohesion, he seems to agree with premodern philosophies that modern people are prone to call "undemocratic," "authoritarian," and "unemancipated" or "unenlightened."

COMMUNITY   The philosophical republic of modern philosophers does not in fact have the pure structure of a contractual association into which each and every member has entered by a completely informed and freely chosen decision. Before a philosopher becomes aware of her belonging to a certain style or tradition, she has already been initiated, trained, and formed in a specific manner. Even if the school where she learned the theory and practice of philosophy offered a variety of styles, she was forced to side with one method or to combine elements of several already existing methods. An absolute beginning is impossible, and even the greatest originality emerges from traditional practices. Despite their ideal of autonomous thought, modern philosophers form a community (encompassing several subcommunities) that combines a general agreement about principles and mission with particular and individual differences. These differences sometimes grow into hostilities, but even then a common orientation can be discovered. More than a freely chosen association, a philosophical community is a sort of family. It has its own genealogy, its founders and heroes, traditions and authorities, standards and standard arguments, canon and orthodoxy, method and exemplary practices.

That even the practice of modern philosophers is not averse to authorities and heteronomous institutions can be easily demonstrated by looking at (1) the role of keynote speakers at conferences, (2) the authority ascribed to recommendations for jobs or publications, (3) the exaggerated respect for references and citations (which often prefers names over arguments), (4) the power of committee and board members in philosophical associations, and (5) the political games played with regard to appointments, programs, and grants. One might respond that the realization of any project or ideal is inseparable from perversions, but can the worldwide republic of philosophers do without any authority at all?

By giving itself a name and recounting its genealogy, a philosophical family distinguishes itself from other families. Sometimes it exaggerates its victories, but it is rarely eager to repeat all its battles of the past. It rather takes its own basic convictions for granted, especially in its regular meetings where it celebrates the memory of past and present heroes. Protected against intrusions, it can then speak the family language in conversations without being questioned incessantly about its axioms and postulates.

A few examples may illustrate this all-too-brief description of philosophical communities that have developed in modernity (and that still mark most of today's philosophical business). When Latin disappeared as an academic language, philosophy became more and more national, and when many people—even professors—no longer deemed knowledge of foreign languages indispensable for education, the provincialism of national philosophies was no longer considered an obstacle for universally valid thought. In some countries ignorance of foreign languages was even encouraged in the name of patriotism. Notwithstanding the claim that philosophy is and should be autonomous and universal, we have come to live in a situation where thinking seems irremediably scattered among French, German, Anglo-Saxon, and other branches of philosophy. Apparently, language, geography, and history have more influence on the mode of universal(?) thought than modernity could foresee and would be willing to accept. Or have national thinkers not thought profoundly and universally enough? Did they betray the modern ideal of autonomous universality, or did their practice refute the forced purity of that ideal?

In addition to splintering into national families, philosophy has also differentiated itself among analytic, phenomenological, existential, feminist, African American, Asian, Christian, Jewish, secular, metaphysical, onto-theo-logical, modern, and postmodern philosophies. All of these names conceal a host of problems. For example, how would it be possible for a philosophy *not* to be analytic, phenomenological, and existential? Further, why should women and African Americans think differently than other thinkers, especially those who share the same culture with them?[14]

The difference between modern and "postmodern" philosophy is, of course, an important issue for the present meditation, but the quasi-temporal qualification of postmodern is hardly helpful for understanding that difference. That those who call themselves or their heroes "postmodern" form a sort of family seems to be a fact, however. Not only do they share an awareness of their having transcended (or "transgressed") the historical stage of modernity, they also uphold a genealogy according to which the entire history of Western metaphysics, as onto-theo-logical, lies definitively behind us, that all grand stories have become impossible, that God is dead, and that all attempts at synthesis have to be replaced with undecidable aporias. Many critical questions can be raised with regard to the notions of metaphysics, being, God, aporia, decision, etc., as presupposed by postmodernists, but these questions are often heard as regressive and "metaphysical" atavisms that only hinder the advancement of thought. If, for example, one points out important holes in the postmodern genealogy of metaphysics, such intervention is seen as rude and as a symptom of bad taste rather than as an invitation to discuss the monumental thought of Plotinus or Aquinas. Perhaps, however, we should not exhaust ourselves by endless criticisms of "metaphysics," but rather be sensitive to post-postmodern attempts to regroup by appealing to great thinkers of all time (including, for example, Aristotle, Plotinus, Aquinas, Cusanus, Pascal, Spinoza, Kant, Hegel, Nietzsche, Blondel, and Bergson) in order to constitute new family relationships through concerted retrievals of slumbering traditions whose vitality is not inhibited by the prejudices of modernity.[15]

From "I Think" to "We Speak"

If the ego that thinks is an abstract element of the life that is lived by someone who can designate him- or herself by the pronoun "I," philosophy cannot avoid reflecting again and again on the mode(s) in which thinking and living involve one another. Is thinking *only* an abstract element, dependent in all its aspects on the lived life from which it emerges? Does it have any power over the life of the thinker? Is the latter, in some respects, ruled by the former or vice versa? How relevant is thought for living, and what light does life shed on thought?

No one becomes a philosopher without initiation. To participate in the business of the philosophical community—with its traditions, classics, ongoing discussions on issues that here and now are preferred over others, etc.—presupposes that I have listened to teachers who spoke to me. All philosophers have been educated by speakers or writers who were already involved in a historical process called "philosophy." The development through which I have made the transition from naïveté to acquaintance has been governed by particular philosophers. These were excellent or mediocre (if they were bad, I have learned something else); they spoke French, German, English, Italian, Spanish, Dutch, or some other language; they liked some classics and schools more than others and had styles and hobbies of their own; they impressed and formed me by their enthusiasm for certain aspects of philosophy and by their specialization in a few topics or authors; but none of our professors mastered the whole range of issues, arguments, theories, and developments that constitute the vast domain of philosophy. My initiation into philosophy was limited by the gates that were guarded by my teachers, even if I, through reading and reflection, have been able to open a few other gates. Beginnings cannot vanish altogether. In becoming what we, as mature philosophers, are, the past has been transformed and perhaps renewed, but never abolished. The teachers to whom we owe our introduction are part of our destiny (which may be a blessing or a curse). Of course, the word *teacher* is not exhausted by the faculty of our schools; we can begin again when startled by a genius or a revolutionary text from elsewhere or another time.

Not merely our education but the entire philosophical practice is accomplished by thinkers who speak to one another or write for readers who, in some way, respond to the offered text. Without speaking, listening, writing, and responding, no philosophy would exist. If the issues and arguments—if the "content" of thought—can neither exist nor be understood without being addressed to listeners or readers, why then have philosophers paid so little attention to the necessity of this fact? The distinction between speaking (writing) and the spoken (written) and their relationship must be analyzed before we can assess the relevance of statements and theories. Metaphilosophy cannot confine itself to the reproduction of monologic egos; the exchange between speakers, on which all theories depend, must show to what extent it is irreducible to any (spoken or written) content and irreducibly relevant for their meaning. This will be the task of our next meditation (chapter 2).

A second line of investigation, to which dissatisfaction with the modern project may invite us, concerns the question: What or who is "ego," and what are speakers or listeners seeking in philosophy? What is the aim, the orientation or the "sought," of thinking, and how does it relate to the "sought" of life? If we discover what ultimately motivates thinking and how thinkers unavoidably address other (potential or actual) thinkers, we might be able to renew philosophy without rejecting its ancient, medieval, modern, or recent past.

TWO

Speaking

Speaking To / Speaking About

Did you say anything? What did you say? You said something to me. Did you say something about something to me? About someone? About me? To me? Did you call me? Greet me? Implore me? Warn me? Insult me?

My first encounters with language occurred when others spoke to me: my mother, perhaps the doctor who delivered me, a nurse, my father, sisters, brothers. As a greeting, it welcomed me into the world. They said something *about* me, while speaking to one another. That touched me only laterally; but in speaking *to* me, they drew my attention, thus orienting my early life.

The world into which I entered is a world of speakers and listeners. Speaking and listening are existentials; no humans exist without them.

Philosophy has analyzed language as an ensemble of propositions, as a structural network of signification, as textuality and contextuality, but rarely has it shown interest in the act of *addressing* through which a speaker directs words to listeners. A classical formula through which philosophers have sought access to the mysteries of language is "saying something about something,"[1] but obviously this phrase offers only a restricted view. It is a formula that concentrates on the content of a specific type of expression (the stating or ascertaining one), but pays little or no attention to the role and the circumstances of the speakers who may say something about something (or someone) and the listeners to whom their speaking is directed. No language exists unless it is mobilized by someone who addresses someone else (*tis legei tini*).

The speaker (nominative) and the one to whom the speaker speaks (dative) are the persons through which all language comes to life; they save it from the fossilizing sleep of death. Their role cannot be eliminated by any insistence upon the (quasi-)independence of language, texts, or literature. Heidegger's famous dictum "language speaks"[2] is simply not true, although a benevolent reading might defend it as a hyperbolic emphasis on the suggestive and pre-dictive power of inherited sayings, proverbs, fables, myths and stories, theories and literature.

It is true that twentieth-century linguistics has extensively studied the contexts and horizons of speech and writing and the various performatives through which users cause changes in others and in themselves, but has the addressing gesture itself—the "to-" or "towardness," the surprising, challenging, and provoking character of the *address*—sufficiently been understood? Does addressing fit at all within the framework of issues that we can study, observe, think *about*, or treat as an object of scientific or philosophical consideration?

No language becomes speech unless addressors and addressees appropriate and actualize its possibilities in their speaking and listening, even if—like Sancho Panza—they add to the world nothing other than repetitions of commonplaces and proverbs. Even such repetitions are unique insofar as they are appropriated and (re-)addressed to others by unique individuals in unique situations. At the very least, the application of commonplaces to a singular and unique here-and-now shows how they can be used in a new way. We will have to meditate on the relations that bind speaking to the unique lives and circumstances of speakers and hearers later, but for now I will focus on speaking as such, all the while emphasizing the difference between that which people speak about (the "*said*," the message or the content) and the *addressing* through which all saids are communicated. Within speaking itself we must then distinguish between the speaker and the listener, while at the same time realizing that they are typically bound together by the communication of a common issue and a common concern that can be said.

You speak to me about something. However, I cannot understand or even hear what you are saying if this event is not preceded by a shared history of speech. Not only have you learned how to speak from other speakers (fathers, mothers, teachers, etc.), but I, the listener, must likewise have been initiated into this history, albeit in a most elementary way. Your message can be minimal, almost nothing—"Hello!" or "Hi," for example, do not confer much content—but even then you affect me, you make contact with me. What mothers say to their babies can be meaningless as far as the content is concerned, but the communicative melody and rhythm of their speaking are essential. The same could be said of some enamored dialogues, in which the tone and gesture of the addressing imply a wordless or "nonsensical" message. A poem may emerge in such a conversation, but it does not seem equivalent to the unspoken hints. Even a trivial expression might do a better job of transmitting the deep interest it refers to than a more elaborate paraphrase—which runs the risk of being forced and inauthentic. After all, the age-old ritual of saying "I love you" is superior to all more elaborate synonyms.

There are many *modes* of addressing: with or without words or gestures, with or without passion, hostility, love, or diplomacy. In all of its modes, however, speaking turns someone toward someone else, thereby bringing them face to face.[3]

When speaking speaks about something, it is bound to the horizons and the context that belong to that something and to the situation in which it is encountered. Speaking itself, your addressing me or my addressing you, cannot be reduced to the issue we speak about or to the situation. It is neither an element of the text or context, nor does it belong to the network of linguistic differences that constitute meaning. Though the latter co-determines the meaning of the communicated message, it is the speaker who offers, presents, directs, and addresses the message, and thus makes himself responsible for it, even if he does not quite know *what* he is saying. The messenger is not an element of the text or of the said and its context. Nor is he its horizon, for he is different from the entire economy that rules the textual and contextual world of phenomena and horizons. Hermeneutics can clarify the composition of this world but not its being offered, proposed, presented, and handed over by the one committed to it.

All interpretations and clarifications of things, events, and texts depend for their meaning upon the speakers or writers who present them as their views or hypotheses. By themselves, these views cannot necessitate any interpreter to appropriate or propose, or even to consider them. They do not exist unless someone decides to accept or produce them as plausible explanations that deserve support. No text draws my attention if it is not supported by someone who convinces me that it deserves to be read. This "someone" is not necessarily another person; it might also originate in me, e.g., as the one who wants to read all the texts of a favorite author. However, the discovery of this author and my decision to read all her works are preceded by a prior presentation in which someone else, perhaps a teacher or a friend, or another author, was involved.

A merely hermeneutical approach can show that many different interpretations of a text are plausible and entitled to respect; it can also lead to indecision and acceptance of provisional or definitive ambiguity, but even so one cannot avoid all kinds of commitment. To insist upon the undecidability of certain alternatives, for example, is a commitment to one overall (or meta-)position, especially when that undecidability is presented and proposed as a not-merely-subjective "impossibility." However, even the hesitant presentation of some thesis or hypothesis by an uncommitted speaker is already a speaking that radically differs from the message it delivers. Speaking and the spoken, writing and the text, saying and the said,[4] are irreducible to one another, though they belong together in an unbreakable union. Only at their limits do they seem capable of a relative independence: wordless speaking is possible, but it replaces or imitates words by other sounds or gestures, while unaddressed words are *legio*, though their need of a reader or presenter belongs to their reality. In any case, speaking as such can be neither understood nor even made an issue by exclusive concentration on the said or the text and their essential characteristics. A phenomenology of speaking is a necessary condition for any study of language. Moreover, if philosophy and science themselves are modes of speaking, thinking about their essence involves us in an analysis of their originating from and issuing into a specific kind of speaking.

You Speak to Me

In speaking to me, you direct your words to me, even if you do not face me. Perhaps you have called me from the Philippines or left a message on my desk, but your presence is evident. Even if you died a long time ago, in your letters you affect me and I see how you looked at me not only then and there, but also—differently—here and now. If you are Plato or Hegel, we have never been familiar with one another, yet you address me in your texts and have been an interlocutor for me during many years. Your texts would not excite me if they did not permit you to speak to me. Reduced to be only texts without authors, they would be mere artifacts, comparable to the fossils of nature or the patterns of crystals and cobwebs.[5] I could still admire and analyze them as interesting and puzzling constellations, but they would need a person who addresses them to me—if not the author, then a reader, teacher, or interpreter—to make me hear them as concerning me.

What does it mean that a speech concerns me, targets me, is addressed and directed to me? When speaking addresses, it *calls*: it tries to make me aware of its address and it competes for my attention. As soon as I hear someone speaking to me, I am aware of no longer being alone, caught in a world that is solely mine and thus free to engage in personal contacts or not. Coming from outside, your speech surprises me and affects me: I am no longer a lonely "I-in-the-world." Indeed, if my being "an I" includes my difference from you and from others (him, her, them), then I was neither (an) ego nor "an I" before someone spoke to me. Being affected by speech might well be the beginning of becoming myself.

To be affected by speech is an enormous surprise: someone terminates my isolation by contacting me. My solitude is broken open by words. I am summoned to listen. I am free to pay attention to the call, but I am no longer free to continue an absolutely private existence. Turning away from the addressing voice, fleeing from the call, refusing to hear it, opposing a stubborn silence to it, or any other reaction are forms of engagement with the caller: they are a *response*.

Speaking is a provocation to respond. It does not let the hearer be free to remain alone and untouched by contact. Because I was born into a world of speakers, I was never alone. I can, of course, *become* lonely by ignoring all the calls for attention that reach me, but I cannot undo the initiatives that provoke me to participation in the conversation.

Speaking calls for hearing and attention—that is, for *listening*. Because I am surprised by being spoken to, a moment of listening seems unavoidable, but I can cover my ears or go away. If I do listen, however, I let myself be provoked into accepting an initial contact, which might develop into a more or less fitting response to the invitation that is contained in the speaker's call.

The tone, the accompanying gestures (the body language of your looks, smiles, movements, and so on), and the messages that qualify your address also qualify the provocation and my response to it. Provocative modes of speaking challenge me in characteristic ways; they delimit a specific field of possible responses and suggest which kinds of response are more or less appropriate. A friendly greeting, for example, suggests a non-aggressive answer, whereas a hostile attack prompts defense, flight, or fighting. Every provocation is suggestive: it reveals that certain responses are fitting, while others are out of the question. To be spoken to in a specific mode is thus to be provoked to an *appropriate* mode of responding. If my sensibility allows me to be not only a good listener, but also a good respondent, then your speaking to me might result in a becoming response. In such a case, then, it is true that speaking generates *appropriation*.[6]

Responding

Your speaking affects me; it causes a particular kind of *affection*. In all affections there is an element of passivity, but this passivity is not contrary to a specific kind of activity. How can we describe and analyze the characteristic affection caused by your speaking to me?

In order to hear you, I must be open to your address. In order to listen, I need to pay attention to your speech. Hearing and listening express my receptive disposition: I am and make myself open to you, to your words, to the mode and the content of your affecting me. Often there is little time or mental space for a choice to welcome your words: before I can decide or even consider the question of whether I should be affected, I am already listening to you, hearing your tone, receiving your message, allowing you to play a part in the theater of my life. I can *stop* listening, but I cannot prevent its impact altogether. My decision not to pursue the contact you established by your initiative is always preceded by a prior moment of affectedness through speech. There is already an, albeit embryonic, element of responding in all hearing: even a hostile speech is met by a moment of reception. As long as your speaking is inviting, I can welcome it. If it is genuinely friendly, I might enjoy it. In general, we can venture to say that being spoken to immediately elicits a certain kind of welcoming or even an element of gratitude. Such gratitude does not necessarily exclude fear or hatred. Even if your tone and message are threatening, their hostility still expresses a more fundamental occurrence: in talking to me you invite me to participate in the economy of human communication, you offer me a role in the linguistic exchange that defines humanity. By offering me a chance to enter into the community of speakers, you give me the greatest of human opportunities, even if you undo this offer (partially or almost entirely) by bringing my very existence into danger. *As long as you speak to me, you prefer not to kill me.*

"Being-in-the-world" is not an adequate name for being human, if "world" primarily refers to natural, instrumental, economic, vital, and other anonymous structures rather than emphasizing the interpersonal and interlocutory adventures of human history. Whatever "world" may mean, we should never forget that it has become "ours," "yours," and "mine" only through its having been presented, given, "proposed" by speakers who introduced us into it by speech.

We were awakened to life as already responding to the call of speakers who offered us access to a network of communication. They roused our openness out of its slumber, provoking us to our own mode of opening up to the universe that their speaking evoked. Because they spoke a particular language and were accustomed to particular modes of living, they represented the universe in peculiar, colored, limited, and to a certain extent, unique ways, urging us to react by integrating at least parts of their manners and opinions into our own. Their urging made our receptivity very active because considerable effort was needed to adopt the surrounding civilization as the basis of our own style of life. In passing from nature to a highly complex culture, we had to transform a common tradition into an individual mode of being human.

How do I make my own what your speaking offers me? Reception precedes both appropriation and rejection. Even the latter presupposes a moment of affection and consideration before I can refuse to pursue our contact. If I give your speaking a chance, it becomes a relevant element of my emotions, moods, practices, fantasies, speeches, writings, and thoughts. If you taught me something important, I will continue to rely on it, having assimilated it as part of my own basic affections and assumptions. There are many variations between complete rejection and complete assimilation; much depends upon the degree of formation that I have already received, but most often—or perhaps always—those who speak to me leave some trace in me. From this perspective, my character is composed by the traces imprinted upon me by others together with the manner in which I have integrated their speaking.

Affectedness by speech always contains the beginning of an answer. Human passivity cannot be altogether separated from reactivity. Even in extreme suffering or agony, for example, we are already reactive—not necessarily by resistance (although our body hardly allows us to do away with it altogether), but minimally by relating to it in a bearable way. When you address me in words, I already begin to formulate an answer by listening to you. I might remain silent, but something like a telling silence or a burgeoning cry is inevitable.

Above I mentioned that every speech, while affecting us, already suggests a more or less appropriate response. Something similar happens in every encounter with a non-personal phenomenon. All phenomena "speak" to us and provoke us to a response. Although the suggestions contained in this speaking set certain limits to the manner in which the affected person is invited to answer, they still leave open a great diversity of reactions. Much depends upon the mood, the education, the understanding, the sensibility, and the willingness of the addressee. A response is constituted by the cooperation of a responding person with an affecting phenomenon. Their cooperation is preceded and partially determined by the context and the situation of their encounter, the character of the phenomenon, and the character of the reacting person. The addressee can welcome or reject the address, but in either case, she interprets and experiences it according to the hermeneutical possibilities at her disposal. These provide her with a limited range of possible responses, some or all of which may not allow for compliance with the suggestions of the address. If a smooth cooperation is not possible, the encounter will take the form of a struggle, even on the most basic level of affection. Then the suggestions meet with a resistance that is due to affective incompatibility, unwillingness, or other limitations. The outcome of this struggle may be a compromise, and this might lead to a transformation of the initial contact; but the struggle might also turn into lifelong hostility. What I cannot avoid, however, is that even the most hostile word forces me to answer by some re-action on my part. Once it has drawn my attention, I give it a chance and allow for some form of contact and influence.

My life is permeated by a multitude of influences. By way of exaggeration we can say that it is the product of all the influences through which my parents and educators have formed me. It is not true that I am able to integrate on my own all the affections, impressions, and sensations through which the world has affected me. My involvement in the world has been mediated by those who brought the world to my attention: they guided my dealing with it, explained its workings, encouraged my participation in it, and offered it to me by their interpretations of its meaning. The idea that human beings could begin as solitary egos who explore the universe in order to possess and master it is unreal. All our involvements are made possible by presentations through which others proposed a certain interpretation of the world to us: their appropriation of the existing culture prepared and co-determined ours. That we are more or less civilized is due to the influence of others; as messengers and mediators, they formed us according to the particular traditions with which they had become familiar. Before we are capable of behaving as freestanding egos, we are already shaped according to particular patterns; we already have a specific character and *style*.

Formation implies that certain possibilities of use, interpretation, practice, and appreciation are realized, while other possibilities are merely opened up and still others impeded or rejected. Through our educators, we have discovered a limited number of possibilities, realizing some of them and discovering that other possibilities are not realistic for us. The particular culture within which we are at home has allowed us to develop an individual mode of being and several possibilities for further development, but (a) we would have remained subhuman if others had not proposed specific ways of dealing with the world, and (b) the possibilities that are now mine are limited. My human universe is a particular one: it is only one possible world alongside others, a possibility that was prepared before I awakened to any world at all, one among the many worlds that are available, since representatives of different traditions present their own versions of "being-in-the-world."

Others have made it possible for me to feel at home in the world. They initiated me to worldly involvement according to the customs, views, and appreciations of their culture and character. In my interpretation of the phenomena and in my commerce with other people, the manners of my educators continue to rule, though they also change. The world they proposed to me—i.e., the way in which they had appropriated their education—has become my world thanks to my appropriation, which, as my work, implies a transformation. This transformation can be small and traditionalist or considerable, progressive, even revolutionary; but nobody can completely erase a once customary past.

If education and appropriation are constitutive for the course of any human life, the first speakers of everyone's life are authorities that cannot be forgotten. The world they represented remains a component of the world that would later on become ours. Their proposals generated the process that led to our actual convictions, practices, feelings, and theories. It is therefore impossible to reduce our dealings with the world to some kind of immediate contact with the phenomena we encounter. Each encounter is already mediated by the speaking of those who have drawn our attention to the things or events that affect us. Both immediate affection and listening, however, are necessary to make my entrance into the world—and along with it my orientation and worldview—possible. "The world" is always a (re)presented and pro-posed world, a "proposition" to which my assent is asked, a proposal, which I can accept, refuse, or change, but no proposal could be accepted if it would not be supported by my own experience and affections. Those who proposed their already ordered, articulated, and interpreted world to me continue to accompany me in my further elaboration of that world; I cannot stop responding to their propositions, even if I turn away from their guidance. My personal history remains populated by fathers and mothers, masters and initiators. And since they likewise have been heirs of preceding generations, our collective history has been dominated by the voices of all who passed on their versions of the tradition. To back their authority, they refer to exemplary representatives of their tradition: the heroes, saints, and classics whose voices, heard in mythical, religious, historical, or literary texts, continue to guide us through new versions of a long tradition.

The universe is a proposal: it belongs, as *said*, to the *saying* that transmits the traditions of a culture. Nobody could assimilate a culture—nobody could be civilized—if history were not kept alive by the voices of those who present and propose specific historical and individual ways of being-in-the-world.

A proposal suggests but it does not force acceptance. My freedom is provoked when someone offers me a possible way to make sense of the puzzling and disturbing world that we have entered. The way in which I respond to the diversity of propositions that try to seduce and guide me represents a new integration of the traditions that were presented. Its originality depends upon each receiver's singular unicity. In this respect, nothing can be predicted except that the most original breakthrough still owes much of its newness to the education it has absorbed.

The role of culture, tradition, and education is not confined to the earliest past of our lives. Far from being merely a story about babies and children, the preceding analysis attempts to capture an aspect of all human temporality. Until we either give up or die, we continue to learn how to deal with the world in which we are involved. We continue to be guided, inspired, taught by paradigmatic men and women, even children perhaps; not only by saints, prophets, masters of spirituality, classics of thought and literature, discoverers, heroes, and great artists, but also by anyone who, in word or deed, confronts us with an as yet unfamiliar or misunderstood view or behavior. Even if we are not "eternal beginners," we should at least recognize that we are never too old to learn.

If we can show that everyone who speaks—even if the message is trivial—has something new and original to say and that each speaking as such reveals something as yet unknown, we can also affirm that every listener has something to learn. If this is the case, then we can also state that the relation between speaking and listening is always an educative relation. In order to explore the validity of this thesis, we must briefly analyze the teacher-pupil relationship and find out whether the general structure of all conversation contains the elements of such a relationship.

Teacher and Pupil

When the teacher speaks, the pupil listens; but a grown-up pupil has developed at least some initiative in finding this teacher, from whose lectures he hopes to learn. Listening is an art and learning demands a lot of effort and several virtues to be effective, but much of the result depends upon the quality of the teachers. As has already been mentioned, we would not have acquired access to the customs and treasures of our culture unless knowledgeable educators presented them to us. Even a bad teacher can help us by making us acquainted with the opinions and the ethos of a culture, e.g., by inviting us to read some famous texts; but a good teacher offers more than a presentation. Besides the knowledge she passes on with didactical skills, she is concerned about the progress of her students and generous in sharing her reflections about the relevance of the content taught.

In her dedication to her job, the teacher is a role model without aiming at being imitated. Her gift is manifold: (1) by speaking she awakens the student to the dimension of her expertise and draws his attention to issues that were not familiar to him, (2) she responds to his desire for learning by sharing her knowledge with him, (3) she urges him to assimilate the information she has taught and to reproduce it in his own unique way (which already alters it), and (4) instead of hoping that he will imitate her, she stimulates his originality by demanding that he transform what she taught into a speaking of his own.

All of these elements of her gift elicit gratitude. If the teacher is good, the pupil will not rest content with mere imitation (which initially may well be a necessary phase); he will become more and more independent in taking responsibility for his own thinking and experimenting. Such independence begins when the pupil, instead of simply reproducing his lessons, asks critical questions or proposes alternative answers to the teacher's questions. It can develop into competition or cooperation or a combination of both, but the traces of the gift can hardly be erased. The pupil's development is the main response to the teacher's speaking; thus, he returns the gift. The fact that both teacher and student are enriched by giving one another the gift of speaking and sharing does not necessarily contaminate their giving with selfish motivations. If gratitude did not ameliorate the grateful person, it would not be a virtue; however, virtue would lose its beauty if "having virtues for myself" is the only motivation for practicing them. Not only does this remove virtue's beauty, but it also perverts virtue into something else, for the aim of virtuousness (i.e., goodness) lies outside of itself. To be good and thus to be a role model is the effect, not the purpose, of devotion to persons, causes, and endeavors.

The phases of learning from a teacher can be summarized in the following sequence: (a) awakening and entering into an unfamiliar dimension; (b) reception and acceptance; (c) exercises in imitation and assimilation; (d) taking possession of the received and assimilated knowledge; (e) integrating the knowledge into one's life and mind; and (f) original re-production of the received, accepted, assimilated, appropriated, and integrated material that was taught. What is not expressed in this list is the teacher's speaking and the student's responding, on which the entire process depends. There is no speaking without spoken "content" or "said." Indeed, but there is also no content or said without speaking. Nothing can speak to me if it is not brought to life by a human voice that calls for my attention. If the teacher instructs me by making me read a text (i.e., a written explanation of the issues she wants me to study), the text cannot be separated from the teacher's voice. Presentation and some (however succinct) interpretation of the text are necessary in order to attract my attention and prompt my engagement with the text. An ensemble of texts does not form a tradition unless they are re-animated *viva voce* by the teachers and readers who present them.

Once we have received a basic formation, we are capable of taking the initiative necessary for choosing which texts we want to read to ourselves and to others, but mere proximity to a text does not lead to any assimilation. Struggling with a text presupposes a real confrontation, and this demands someone who seduces me to engage with it. The same is true of the interpretations of a text (e.g., a passage from the Bible or Aristotle's *Metaphysics*). To interest me, the interpretation must be presented by someone who makes it a part of her speaking to me; it must be *given* to me in a much more emphatic sense than the one we tend to hear in "the given." Textuality, intertextuality, and tradition require reanimation—a new breath or inspiration—through which new speakers can reach new readers and respondents. Without voices that affect receptive listeners, no message can produce a new generation of educated individuals. Cultural procreation is the result of a marriage between available interpretations and living speakers who take responsibility for them while addressing their audience.

Insofar as it gathers teachers and pupils into dialogues, the process of civilization is characterized by a specific temporality. A teacher represents the tradition of a culture that is already established and brings the past of "the ancients" to new life in order to enable pupils to transform the presented past into a future—which then again will become traditional, thus generating other pupils who become teachers, and so on. "Immortality through procreation?"[7] The time of teaching is a partial answer to the inexorability of death. I learn in order to become a teacher for others (even if teaching will not be my profession). Appropriation cannot be the end, because enjoyment of what I possess does not fully answer the question of why and for what I live. I would hardly enjoy what I have made my own if I could not express it and thus communicate it to others. All that has been said to me must be re-said by me; it urges me to speak out about the heritage that fascinates me. Giving what I have confers meaning onto that which I possess. Amassing wealth suffocates me rather than freeing me.

Learning is the beginning of fecundity. Because I am educated, I cannot refrain from passing on the tradition, even if, by giving out what I have appropriated, I make myself progressively superfluous. "To live for a time after my death" is ambiguous: while it can indicate the greatest generosity, it can also be the title for a narcissistic self-reference without any other future than a name. If such a name is accompanied by inspiring work, the author is generous despite herself. Gratitude is due because her world is greater than her intentions. In any case, the work needs other minds and wills to keep it alive as a promise of new life.

Listening Is Learning

The preceding analysis of the teaching-learning relationship was triggered by the question of whether all dialogue contains certain elements of such a relation. If we concentrate exclusively on that which is said or spoken about (the said), the first impulse might prompt us to deny that the listener always learns something. Do we not hear much too much talking from which we do not learn anything? Do we not read too many texts that repeat what is already known? Each speaker and each listener is unique, however, and their encounter is always an event.

When a speaker communicates something new, a listener can learn, but even previously thought contents are not wholly known insofar as they are expressed anew by a unique person in the unique situation of a conversation with other unique persons. These contents are both perceived and (re)shaped by unique listeners in a unique situation. The unique articulation that common knowledge receives through its being expressed in the speaker's personal style is a version that has not been heard before. It affects the listener in a way that may stimulate her differently than other versions. Learning is a more obvious element of a conversation, however, when entirely new information is offered. This does not necessarily lead to assimilation and integration by the listener—he might disagree with the presented view—but at least he "learns" what the speaker thinks about questions that could be answered in a different way. A great deal of the information we receive consists of beliefs and theories that are worthwhile to know, although we doubt their truth or resist them because of our own convictions. The pluralism of cultures and convictions that characterizes today's world civilization has ruined the ideal of a universally valid interpretation of human life and world, but it has not been able to extirpate our orientation to universal truth. Universality must be sought on another level than that of propositions that can be formulated in universally underwritten declarations. The truth itself hides in the startling and partially conflicting manifold of *proposed* convictions that have not led, and perhaps will never lead, to commonly shared positions. It is possible to understand this plurality, notwithstanding its contradictions, as the contemporary expression of a hidden truth that defies simplifications. By inviting us to further exploration of its protean diversification, the truth urges us to find our way in the labyrinth of its more or less authentic versions, instead of clinging to the one that has become so familiar that it seems to be the only obvious way of being true. If this interpretation of pluralism is correct, new information on an issue could contribute to a better understanding of the issues we share with other people. To that extent, then, we should be eager to "learn" about views and valuations that differ from our establishment.

In the preceding lines we focused on the content or "said" through which a speaker communicates with a listener. However, the question of newness and learning points in another direction when we focus on the speaking itself. Even if the proposed content is minimal, the exchange between the speaker and the listener is unique, not only and not primarily because of the communicated message, but even more so because of each one's unrepeatable individuality (expressed in but not exhausted by their different character, style, personal adventures, birth, and death) and the unique confrontation of their unique destinies. Their unicity can be seen and heard in their faces and voices; it is sensed in listening to the other's speaking. Indeed, "the saying" itself—your addressing me in words or otherwise—is the primary news that cannot be replaced with or represented by anything else—and certainly not by "language" or any accumulation of "saids."

By speaking or writing *about* your unique speaking to me, I make it disappear. I perceive it only so long as I undergo its provocation. It cannot be reduced to an element of the text (or the "economy") of the world, because it belongs to another dimension than the network of all realities and relations that can be talked about. It thus cannot be defined or delineated as distinct from other parts of the world, but only referred to as immediately experienced in a unique kind of affection.

The uniqueness of the other's speaking permeates the entire "said" it communicates. Even if the other repeats a current interpretation of things, this repetition is different from earlier versions because it is proclaimed from the perspective of a unique and uniquely situated person in a unique situation who addresses others having their equally unique identities within their own unique situations. Though all the individuals involved can agree on many generalities, the universality concretized in their distinct positions cannot encompass the manifold unicities of the interlocutors who share it. It is impossible to shove away the latter as accidental or contingent in order to concentrate only on universally valid truths. For the entire realm of such truths depends on their being voiced and addressed by those who discuss them with one another. The truth of their discussion cannot be found without turning to the truth of the dimension revealed in their facing, speaking, challenging, and turning toward one another, while at the same time sharing a universalizable universe. Perhaps it is precisely that non-universalizable, yet constantly occurring truth of unicities in dialogue, which is the most important event, more important than a general agreement about that which is or should be talked about.

The challenge through which a teacher affects me provokes me to speak in my turn, partly repeating, partly transforming the message I receive. In this way, tradition remains alive; the history of its transformative repetitions is ruled by the interplay of (re-)creative fidelity,[8] always endangered by distortions and perversions, but also supported and encouraged by faithful reconstructions of the original intents. Fundamentalist attempts to maintain the letter against the inevitability of contextual transformations are suspicious of those who try to combine loyalty with real life. But would any of them be sufficiently motivated if they were not provoked by speakers who spoke *to* them—and who in some, albeit weak, sense deserve the name "prophet"? Just like lives, traditions die when they are not put to the test by surprisingly new adventures. Adventures are unpredictable, so it is impossible to deduce the future of a tradition or of any past in general. Clinging to the letter of the past or swearing by the convictions of the present impedes the future, and thus paralyzes inspiration. A good antidote against such perversions can be found by attending to the living presence of the "prophets": in turning their face and addressing their word to us, they remind us of our own responsibility for all that we have learned. Indeed, having been educated, we are no longer mere listeners; our version of the tradition should be worthy of being taught to other generations in other times and other places.

Again, the metaphors of fecundity, procreation, and generation present themselves to a description of the interpersonal time to which traditions owe their transformative perdurance. Plato saw the connection between teaching and learning as an erotic relationship (and not as a deduction) and its result as an overcoming of mortality.[9] Must we still defend the thesis that *eros*, in a qualified sense, is more originary than the search for certifiable truth? Is the fact of a conversation more desirable and important for human lives than the issue that is spoken about? If the full truth that assembles all people remains hidden and scattered in the many attempts to capture it, is it then not more important to participate in the conversation as responsibly as one can, rather than grasping the truth in one of its more or less certified but biased versions?

Dialogue

A pupil becomes a teacher when he has learned enough to educate others. When a listener answers a speaker, he is or begins to be a colleague by taking responsibility for presenting positive or negative or interrogative observations to the one who first instructed him. As interlocutors, you and I have entered a relationship that has its own type of exchange and temporality. Both of us live our own time, but these times are combined and unified as long as our exchange perdures. Each of us retrieves a unique past in a unique present from out of the perspective of a desirable future, but our dialogue relies on a unique situation, which, at the same time, it co-determines. Since we are mortal, nothing of the future is guaranteed, except that it stops somewhere; part of the past is factual, but its full meaning is delayed; the time of initiatives is the present. The main question you and I must answer is: how should and how will we transform our past into a future? Because I am responsible not only for my own present and future, but also for our exchange, I co-determine at the same time the courses of my own and your life, while you participate in mine.

A conversation between you and me would not be possible if we did not share certain existential and cultural elements, which in turn are reshaped by our communication. Having become attentive speakers and vocal listeners, we have established a certain level of equality (even if you are more knowledgeable or more interesting than I). We alternate in giving and receiving messages according to certain procedures, thereby maintaining a dialogue that honors the essential features of speaking (such as awakening, provocation, etc.), listening (reception, assimilation, etc.), and answering, as was indicated above. Hence, the relationship in which we are caught demands the practice of specific virtues: attention, respect for the other's words even if they are not fully adequate, patience in letting the other speak and finish speaking, humility in recognizing one's own need for instruction, and so on. Arrogance and impatience destroy all conversation, whereas nonviolent, just, and friendly words replace war with dialogue. A conversation is not a mere work of art; it presupposes moral action. And action presupposes freedom.

That we are free does not mean that you or I are the complete origin of the fact and the content of our actions. After modernity it should be clear that human freedom primarily awakens and continues to operate by *responding* to the human civilization into which we are born and educated. Whatever Nietzsche may have thought about reactivity, it is nothing to be ashamed of if it expresses the originary acceptance that characterizes all selfhood.[10] You are free to the extent to which you integrate and transform the heritage that you have received. While you share almost everything with those who have learned how to be and behave in a human way, your mode of being shows how you have chosen to share the common property of your community. The freer we are, the more original we are in sharing, reacting, competing, cooperating, producing, and generating. Such freedom does not have to be extraordinary; it can be enacted in a quite conventional way, but even then it displays a strong self or will.

Insofar as you and I share a common culture, tradition, or heritage, we are *with* one another: a *we* in the rigorous sense of an—albeit very small—community. Heidegger's *Mitsein* and *Mitdasein* and his explanation of language as *Mitteilung*[11] can be illustrated by analyses of such sharing. The nuclear community composed by you and me can easily be extended: we can invite others ("them") to join our being-together-and-united in sharing one and the same tradition. Being-with does not have sharp boundaries; it can be as wide as humanity or be restricted to continents, nations, linguistic or religious communities, and the "republics" of science, literature, or philosophy.

While sharing is presupposed, it is not enough for a dialogue. Our face-to-face cannot be reduced to any "we," although our forming a "we" is presupposed and kept alive by a dialogical relationship. Emmanuel Levinas has tirelessly pointed out that you and I originally do not appear as equal: you emerge for me as high; the dimension revealed in your looking at me or speaking to me is the dimension of "height," "the infinite" and "the absolute."[12] To show this, Levinas emphasizes the moral absoluteness of the command that regards me or speaks to me in the naked, vulnerable, powerless, but infinitely obligating face of the Other. The other's height and infinity are not restricted to their moral character—they also have an immediately religious signification—but I will not pursue this line of questioning here. Taking for granted Levinas's descriptions, I will focus on a slightly different question and draw upon other distinctions to clarify the exceptional relevance of your speaking to me with regard to the "economic" relations between persons and things.

Levinas's descriptions of height, obligation, service, substitution, and suffering for others are frequently misunderstood as variations on the theme of lordship and servitude, treated by Hegel and misinterpreted by Kojève, or even as a retrieval of Aristotle's theory about the relations that link master and slave.[13] Such relations connect people insofar as they play different roles within the networks of mutual exchange in the dimensions of action, labor, property, buying and selling, praising and punishing, competing and supporting, fighting and cooperating. The totality of these dealings can be explained as an "economy"[14] ruled by specific conditions, laws, and expectations. According to the rules of their roles, the persons involved are expected to act in a more or less predictable way; when they do not conform to the normal patterns, they are called to order because erratic behavior derails the system. One important rule—or rather a metarule—prescribes reciprocity: when you work for me, I have to compensate you, for example by paying you a salary. This rule seems to be universal; it even holds sway in many forms of giving, as the institution of potlatch shows. Hegel's analysis of human encounter on the most primitive level includes a good deal of violence, but even this violence is ruled by a rational necessity. I am tempted to kill another human being because he threatens my monopoly; but if I am not strong or cunning enough to do that, I must fight. In the fight I can choose to risk dying in order to remain sovereign; but if I lack the courage to take that risk, I must either flee (accepting that the world should be divided in two), or I must become the servant of the other, who then, if he does not flee, becomes the lord. In each phase, one's way of acting confronts the other with a limited alternative. If I fight courageously, you must also fight and one of us must die, unless you surrender your freedom to me and become my valet or slave. If you surrender yourself, I can still kill you, but in doing so, I would preempt all the meanings that could have emerged from our encounter: I would then continue to be alone, forfeiting all profit from your words and works. The initiatives involved in the struggle between two competitors are responses to actions that offer only very restricted alternatives for choice. The economy of their struggle is comparable to a chess play: only so many moves are possible and any move restricts the number of possible responses. As participants in an economy—whether social, utilitarian, political, linguistic, or other—we are caught in a web of limited alternatives. The totality of moves and reactions that are possible in a certain economy form a particular world in which our roles can be defined as elements of an overall system. From this (economic) perspective, all human actions and reactions appear to be modulations of a universal pattern that is ruled by the "invisible hand" of some anonymous power. This power leaves some space for human freedom, but it predetermines the alternatives from which we must choose.

It is the great merit of Levinas to have fought the belief that all persons, things, and events are entirely caught in the structures and rules of a universal "economy"—the "world"—by pointing to the face as an irruption that cannot be placed, related, caught, understood, or treated as an element of such a universe. Presupposing that an economic universe or world can be characterized as finite and relative, he calls the face "absolute" and "infinite." Instead of being a phenomenon that fits into a system, the other who speaks is exceptional and unique: a "revelation." Not being an element of some whole (but still surrounded by and linked to several wholes), the Other comes toward me "from on high," from an elsewhere that is not worldly in the economic sense.

Confronted with the Other in you—i.e., face to face with you as (my) Other—I perceive you as high and myself as looking up, summoned to a response that does justice to your "highness." The difference between your highness and my lowliness is entirely different from the difference between a master and a slave, however. The lordship that you reveal to me, your servant, commands me to welcome you and be hospitable to you, to feed, help, console, and promote you, *because of your being you*: this concrete and unique Other whom I happen to encounter. The law of this encounter does not condemn me to be your slave, nor does it fix you into the role of a master; rather, it defines all relations between two persons, each of whom is I as well as you. Indeed, as soon as two persons meet, *both* experience themselves as (an) "I am faced by you," at the same time knowing that you are experiencing me the same way. In contrast to Levinas's conviction that mutuality is excluded from this experience, I maintain that we cannot avoid being aware of the fact that *each* I (including you) experiences the Other's ("your") face (including mine) as irruptive, demanding, obligating, infinite, and absolute. I thus know that you likewise perceive me as obligating you to welcome and serve me. However—and herein I share Levinas's concern for maintaining the difference between the order of the "infinite" (or absolute) and the economic dimension of systematic exchange—my obligation to be "for-you" does not at all depend upon your fulfilling the obligation my face imposes on you. My and your obligations toward the Other *do not originate in any act of will but simply in your and my being a human Other* (i.e., "a you"). The Other's absoluteness (as revealed in you for me and in me for you) must be recognized. You, as much as I, must enact this recognition in practice, but the relations between my humility toward your lordship and your service to me should not be understood as descriptions of our equality in being human, rational, willing, and so on. Instead, they intersect as two asymmetric relations, which, through the inequality of their direction, constitute our (unequal) equality: your face commands me, while my face commands you. Our equality originates in the dissimilarity of contrary demands: while I perceive you as my lord or lady, you see me as your lady or lord. Both of us are one another's lord or lady. You and I are bound together by the chiasm of two identical but opposite inequalities. This mutual or chiastic asymmetry is the source of respect, politeness, regard, service, dedication, devotion and compassion.

A dialogue, then, presupposes sharing as well as a double inequality between you and me. Both conditions have moral aspects that make them fundamental for any ethics. But even on a morally neutral level (which, of course, is an abstraction), they found the sharing and the difference between high and low that are characteristic for all kinds of teaching, instruction, training, and informing. As we have already said, some form of teaching and novelty is involved in any dialogue: you and I alternate in surprising and informing one another, at least by the unique manner of our speaking. Alternately giving and receiving, we promote or debase one another to the extent to which we respond positively or negatively to the call for respect that is implicit in your and my speaking.

From Dialogue to Conversation

"Dialogue" can neither be the last nor the first word about speaking. For you and I cannot isolate ourselves from the many others who are present at our exchange. "They," the others, precede, support, and succeed what happens between us, and we would not be able to say anything without borrowing from them.

That "they" condition our dialogue is obvious when we remind ourselves of the instruction we had to receive before we could speak and say something interesting. However, "they" are also our present and future: not only do you and I talk about common issues in a way that is understandable for others, we are also aware of our responsibility for those who can interrupt our dialogue by appearing on the scene. Since the law of the face, which demands attention and respect, originates in the face as such (and not in any action, convention, or decision), every potential speaker has the same right to enter a dialogical relationship with me. This is enough to condemn all attempts to seal off our dialogue against all participation by others. Without excluding the possibility of a dyadic intimacy or confidential consultations, the existence of others makes you and me also responsible for them. By facing me, they invite me to enter into a dialogue in the same way you invited me or responded to my invitation. When they face you and me while we talk to one another, they demand a role in our dialogue. By allowing them to participate in our exchange, we widen it to a polylogue, whose rules are different from the duological exchange between you and me. Many configurations can now emerge, depending upon the number, the interests, the language, the education, and the character of the participants. The more people a dialogue involves, the more its exchange needs organizational rules and skills; the more it also becomes a world of communication with an economic character of its own.

Between dialogue and economized communication, a complex process of conversation occurs, in which face-to-face relationships alternate and intermingle with less personal, more communitarian relations. Insofar as others are allowed to personally and actively intervene in a dialogue that started as an exchange between you and me, they are welcomed as other yous. Thus, they multiply the dyadic relationship between you and me. Other others, however, though acknowledged as potential participants, are left out or prefer to withdraw (e.g., because they are involved in dialogues of their own) and thus remain silent or even invisible for me.

We can attempt a classification of the others ("they") who are present to a dialogue between you and me. We already mentioned (1) the mothers and fathers and the instructors who initiated us into the culture of (2) the communities whose members we have become. They acquainted me with the mixture of good and evil that composes our heritage. Through it, we remain in touch with the words and works of (3) the ancients and (4) those who transmitted our tradition(s). Since we are not able to inherit anything unless our inheritance is passed on to us by re-presenting speakers, all of these mediators elicit gratitude, though we might meet the evil aspects of our tradition with immediate or delayed feelings of guilt and anger. Insofar as your and my language is not confined to private utterances, our dialogue is also open to (5) all who wish to overhear it. Moreover, through you, who listen to me, I indirectly reach (6) your other interlocutors, and you do the same through me. Thus, directly or indirectly we influence (7) colleagues and (8) future generations.

The overall conversation of which a dialogue is only a fragment encompasses many anonymous interpretations and hermeneutical processes, but nothing would happen—there would not be any human history—if cultures, traditions, mores, and opinions were not appropriated, proclaimed, transformed, and passed on by living speakers who fulfill their pro-phetic task. *Your*—a representer's—address is necessary to awaken, surprise, affect, touch, initiate, form, challenge, and motivate every "*me*" who enters the universe. It is true that parts of your task can be gradually taken over by my own self, insofar as this develops into a conscience, but without the challenge of a "you" who provoked that development, my conscience would not awaken to its own responsibility. As conscience, however, the self functions as "my prophetic soul": its mature voice sets the standards for my future.

The ongoing conversation through which individuals, communities, traditions, languages, cultures, and civilizations communicate cannot be reduced to exchanges (competition, conflict, osmosis, integration, and so on) between anonymous interpretations or ideologies; beside the economy of impersonal processes, the conversation presupposes the living voices of personal addressing and responding.

Only "correspondence" between irreplaceable persons who expose themselves to one another as you and me can prevent the conversation from stopping or turning into the mindless repetition of computerized commonplaces. Face-to-face relationships—especially those cultivated in various forms of friendship—are thus indispensable for conversations to live, and thus for the continued life of traditions and communities. Since life implies transformation, an analysis of the conversation cannot stop at a consideration of the conflicts and fusions of interpretative traditions; it also must focus on the inevitable and life-preserving changes and mutations that are due to the living speakers who make themselves responsible for them.

If face-to-face encounters of unique speakers who listen and respond to one another are indispensable, "the conversation" cannot be understood as a plurality of monological positions. As *proposals*, each position is pro-posed by someone who (as parent, teacher, friend, or colleague) addresses others who, in turn, are urged to respond by making that proposition their own through interpretation, understanding, and a choice between integration, rejection, or transformation. Whatever the receiver decides, she will again address others when she proposes the result of her reaction in the form of a new (re)interpretation. When she realizes that the speaker whose proposition made her respond to it was not an absolute beginning, but equally a receiver who retrieved an earlier address, she discovers how much we owe to the "prophets" who made our belonging possible. At the same time her responsibility for those who come afterward becomes obvious: all of her speaking will urge her addressees to respond by a new personalization of her message, which then turns into a new and "prophetic" transmission. Of course, this sketch of traditional filiation is much too simple to do justice to the many forms of transmission, objection, rejection, amendment, modification, rebellion, reform, revolution, and so on; it is important, however, to underline the irreducible role of the individual speakers in the history of meaning and interpretation. Hermeneutics cannot be complete unless it respects the originary status of the prophets. Similarly, a philosophy of dialogue and conversation misses its main issue when it forgets:

(1) the irreducibility of individual speakers;
(2) the address as a fundamental relationship that "precedes" and supports all other linguistic structures;
(3) the relations that tie speakers and listeners together (a) as members of communities and participants in common traditions and (b) as facing one another in relations of you and me;
(4) the "republic" of all speakers who seek and proclaim meaning in response to the "propositions" they received; and
(5) the affinity created by the various kinds of their belonging together and the hope that somehow their ways of seeking and proclaiming might converge or lead to a later convergence.

Hermeneutics and/or Conversation?

If presentation, by way of proposal and proposition, is an essential element of all that is said and heard, and if individual unicity is essential for every presentation, both the egological conception of language and its reduction to the anonymity of a system must be abandoned. Not only is interlocution essential for every proposition, but all meaningful speaking and writing implies individual responsibility. Even proverbs and laws must be personalized before they can be effective; no word is possible without audience and at least some people must take responsibility for its concretization.

With regard to the pluralism of interpretations through which individuals and communities have tried to make sense of their existence, the hermeneutical theories of the nineteenth and twentieth centuries have proposed meta-standpoints from which pluralism can be understood as having some kind of coherence or necessity. By taking responsibility for such an overview, each of those meta-theories risks understanding itself as an encompassing and final monologue—unless it offers itself as a tentative meta-proposal calling for dialogue on a higher level of discussion, critical transformation, or outright destruction. No theory is complete unless it is diversified by unique and original recipients; their unavoidable otherness necessarily makes a difference. But rather than leading the polylogue into an impasse, this "differentiation" harbors the possibility of a more promising commerce with truth than the idea of a monological system that rules modern philosophy.

THREE

Philosophy as Conversation

Sharing and Originality

If we are engaged in philosophical conversations, we owe this to our teachers who, before us, were already at home in the world of philosophy. To what extent is this "world" not only a culture but also a community?

In any case, we cannot doubt that philosophy's institutions and rituals condition its discussions. If the world of philosophy constitutes a community, our contributions express membership. However personal and original someone's thinking might be, it emerges from a wider context composed by former experiences and thoughts. An accurate description of such contexts and our dependence on them needs the contributions of several human sciences, but even without professional competence in psychology, sociology, and history, we may venture a sketch of the characteristic economy in which one must be at home before being able to propose a personal thought.

Insofar as philosophy preexists individual philosophers, it is dominated by a typical constellation of leading opinions and interpretative grids and by a general ethos that may encompass several sub-ethoses. Attached to their own heroes and heritage, a few traditions are dominant, whereas others are deemed outdated or marginal. Each epoch has its own orthodoxies and these are enforced through educational institutions and leading figures who have enough power to appoint or dismiss other leaders. Many philosophers, especially young ones whose careers are not yet secure, try to adjust their work to the judgment of the established powers, at least provisionally or in appearance.

The philosophical life of the early twenty-first century is not ruled by the same institutions as, for example, those of the thirteenth or the late eighteenth century or by those of Plato's *Akademia* and Aristotle's *Lykeion*, but their impact is as undeniable. In large parts of the Western hemisphere the procedures of initiation, evaluation, hiring, tenure, and promotion are regulated quite rigidly, although surprises and exceptions are possible. The communal aspect of philosophy is expressed in schools and associations, and celebrated in conferences and meetings, where its conversational aspect is most often reduced to some questions and answers, although once in a while a more substantial confrontation is organized. Though teamwork and interdisciplinary projects are favored in theory, the modern model of the lonely thinker is still a reality, even if we recognize that all originality is heavily dependent on tradition and communal conditions.

The temporality of contemporary philosophy is manifest in its handling of the traditions that it—aware or unaware—prolongs. Some schools believe that their progressive advancement has left all pasts behind, but most thinkers are well aware that creative retrieval is the only way of passing from old to future wisdom. As much as other parts of human culture, philosophy is bound to repeat and transform its heritage in order to not only possess but also hand it over to another generation. Moreover, thinking can isolate itself neither from religious and other beliefs, nor from art, sciences, and social or political developments.

With regard to the customs and regularities that (co-)determine the philosophical life, human sciences can sharpen our insight in the social and cultural conditions of individual thought, but they can neither replace the thinkers themselves nor reduce them to fully determined elements of a collective machinery. What, then, is that "instance" or "element" or "source" that makes thinking personal and original? If we cannot answer this question, how could we continue to speak about dialogue or conversation? Would these words then not cover up the disappearance of all freedom (and thus of initiative, creativity, promising, and personal wisdom)?

Before attempting an answer, let us turn to the question of what, more precisely, philosophers are thinking and speaking about, why they are fascinated by their questions, and how they approach their issues. Such a detour might ease our discovery of the originality that is presupposed in all forms of thoughtful speaking.

Issues

What are philosophers talking about? Three answers have dominated philosophy's history: (1) the universe, (2) human existence, and (3) the unity of (1) and (2). As always, these answers are not interesting unless their philosophical motivation(s) can be exposed.

That philosophy differs from all sciences by its scope has been affirmed since Parmenides, who oriented Western thinking by concentrating on *ta panta* (all "things") and *to pan* (the universe), while asking what characterizes their all-encompassing truth. The *being* (*einai*) of all things seemed to be the answer and remained the basic issue for many centuries of cosmic and trans-cosmic or meta-physical thought. That "being" (*einai, ousia, esse*) in modern times was replaced by universality or even by reason and rationality can only be understood in connection with the dominant role human subjectivity began to play; however, this fact cannot hide its affinity with the ontological tradition from which philosophy had emerged. For both versions of the Western tradition—the more ontological and the more anthropocentric one—the human universe was the horizon and the main object of philosophical thought. It seemed to exclude nothing and any other—more limited—object would urge the thinker to transcend it together with all other parts of the universe in order to understand them as particular and individual instantiations of one totality.

According to Heidegger, Western metaphysics has been obsessed by the question of the essence and the structural whole of *ta onta* (beings). Totally absorbed by concentration on the beings that constitute the universe, philosophy forgot the more profound question of being itself, to which all beings owe their being. Some admirers of Heidegger suggest that metaphysics belongs to the past, but how then is it possible to escape or to forget the horizon of the universe-as-experienced-by-(wo)man? Even if the all-encompassing horizon of the ultimate totality poses unconquerable problems for logic and ontology, it seems completely arbitrary to limit philosophy to one or more fragments or to a transcendental question that does not take the totality of the universe into account.

Insofar as metaphysics thinks about the being of human and all other beings, it cannot be abolished; but can we reasonably ask what "being" (or "is") "itself" and the "granting" and "giving" of being *is*? Prima vista it seems all right to ask what "being" or "to be" (or "is") means, but several objections against the very question of the meaning and being of being can be made. In the first place, it is not immediately clear whether the word "being" has one meaning or rather assembles different meanings that cannot be reduced to any unity. Secondly, if "being in general" has one meaning, this can only be so thin and almost empty that it seems to coincide with "nothing" in the sense of "nothing specific"—or perhaps with nothing more than a generic concept that excludes all specific differences (which then cannot be). Thirdly, "the meaning of being" is not equivalent to "the being of being" or the "is-ing" of "is"—if these latter expressions have a meaning at all. Does "being" coincide with appearing, being given, emerging, existing, being real, being only possible, being universal, being here and now, being unique, being present, being temporal or eternal or both, being nothing specific, not even generic? The fact that "being" can be specified, as the former sentence seems to demonstrate, appears to imply its plurality as well as its universality. But "being" cannot be a genus and its differences cannot have the character of various species. However, some sort of being's universality seems inevitable, unless the word "being" covers up a scattering of meanings so radical that it would refute altogether the Parmenidean point of departure and its ontological posterity.

Whatever the answer may be—the universe (the totality of all beings), human existence, the possible or real mode(s) of being something, or being itself—the human universe remains the horizon of any thinker who does not see convincing reasons for restricting it from the outset to one (or some) of its parts or aspects or to transcend it to "something" trans-universal. Can such reasons emerge from further reflection?

The Thinker

Attention to the thinker might further our search for the main issues of philosophy. Amazement about the being of all things can hardly overlook the importance of the thinking subject itself. All questions would disappear if the thinkers fell away. How does thinking relate to other aspects and activities of a philosopher? To what extent does thinking coincide with living or existence in the emphatic sense that was popularized by existentialism?

Each life needs truth. Not omniscience, for there are many sorts of things that can be known, which are, in the end, indifferent and superfluous. The truth we need concerns "the heart of the matter," and this responds to a desire that is the heart of human hearts. Existential truth—may we still call it "wisdom"?—is not a privilege of philosophers; yet philosophy can be understood as a characteristic stylization of that cordial desire for truth. Neither existential nor philosophical thought are eager to know everything about everything, but a certain kind of curiosity may favor an inventive search for the truth that matters. Philosophy is more than a game when it mobilizes its potential for an answer to the questions of human life itself.

Life is more than philosophy, insofar as it can succeed without participation in philosophical discussions; but philosophy offers a strategy of its own for the clarification of decisive questions. Professional thought risks becoming so self-contained that it forgets the quest for wisdom from which it springs, but the quest needs critique and periodical readjustment. Philosophy is only one possibility of searching truth, but once caught by it, one cannot persist in separating it from life itself.

Both thinking and the human existence from which it emerges are moved and motivated by Desire. Thought is oriented primarily toward a true and good, i.e., truly desirable, way of life. Consequently, the motivation of philosophy is fundamentally ethical; its interest in the universe is existentially and ethically oriented. Its motivation thus protects philosophy from falling into mere curiosity. We still focus on the universe—philosophy remains universal—but the universe is centered around human existence insofar as this needs truth in order to be lived well. This insight does not forbid us to examine how, for instance, dogs and mosquitoes or elephants experience space and time, but all relevant questions refer directly or indirectly to human interests. In this sense, all reality—the universe as a whole and the being of all things in it—is thematized in its being-(relevant/interesting/necessary/meaningful/desirable)-for-us. Even the expression "thing-as-it-is-in-itself" refers to something that remains partially hidden and unknown to us. What we know about it is its presumed, postulated, referred to, evoked, invoked, real, possible, or imaginative existence and the unknowability of some or many of its characteristics (which may or may not be known by some non-human subjects).

If Desire drives all human existence, it founds the subjective universality of thinking about the human universe. It creates a commonality of interest in existential, and therefore philosophical, truth and wisdom, even if this does not warrant any answer to the questions involved.

A second form or level of universality has been proclaimed by modern thought, as we have seen above: reason was presumed to be identical and autonomous in all human individuals. In its purest form—not contaminated by contingent authorities, schools, or personal biases—reason was deemed the guiding principle of all thinkers who could abstract their mind from historical intricacies in order to restrict their thinking to the data and laws that rule a non-situated, impersonal, and unhistorical mind, which, for some reason, we could continue to call "ego" or "I." At the same time, however, this abstract ego was deemed to be the subject of the real, historical, monolingual (or insofar as Latin was still used, duo-lingual) contributions to thought written down by Western European individuals so diverse as Hobbes, Descartes, Spinoza, Leibniz, and Kant. Each of them had to protect himself against the admixtures that would contaminate the pure rationality that constituted the philosophical core of their minds. Why this element was identified as an "I" has remained a mystery. Was it not precisely this universal feature that resisted any substantial difference between the thinkers involved? The words "I" or "ego" apparently no longer indicated the differences between you or him or her or them and me, but rather an indistinct, universally identical, absolutely impersonal subject without history supposedly able to take a distance from all inter-individual differences that constitute her as only her, him as only him, you as only you, and me as only me.

The entire truth of which humans are capable had to be contained in each ego's single mind, but the mind no longer coincided with a concern for the historically situated truth sought for by unique and uniquely situated individuals. This turn implied a neglect of all education in traditions of wisdom and denied the necessity of keeping a common heritage alive by handling it on to heirs who would both conserve and renew it through retrieval.

In chapter 2 we have seen how real individuals, in their struggle for truth, are bound, partially determined, internally related, associated, and communalized by innumerable connections to other individuals, and especially how none of them ever stops learning from others living in the past and present. In light of the existential structures by which thinking is determined, the idea of autonomous egos can still be defended as an abstract ideal, if we can show that all relational conditions and determinations may be reduced to expressions of an initially hidden, but ultimately revealed reason itself. However, none of the historical philosophers has ever shown how such an ideal could be realized. That it is a fascinating (even if utopian) ideal cannot be denied by those who are passionately engaged in radical reflection. However, even if it were realizable, we should not neglect the historical reality of another, more existential than dreamed philosophy.

That modern philosophers have not identified without ado the rational ego with the factual or existential ego is testified by their distinction between the empirical or phenomenal ego on one hand, and the transcendental ego that rules, illuminates, constitutes, or otherwise dominates the former, on the other. The question of whether such a transcendental ruling or constitution indeed refers to any kind of ego, and if so, what then the egoic (and not "you-ic," "he-ic," "she-ic," or "we-ic") aspect or structure of this transcendental power is, has not been answered. The hypothesis of such an "ego" appears especially doubtful when it becomes clear that no ego can be conscious of itself without referring to a "you" or "him" or "her" or "us" or "them," and when one is asked to explain how a transcendental ego can be ego-ic without referring to any "you." In other words, please explain how a transcendental ego can speak, or if it cannot, how we can speak in its name. Whatever worth all these abstractions may have for the understanding of our position in the universe and of the universe as fathomed by an individual *cogito*, they must never be hypostasized or separated from their rooting in the concreteness of individual and unique, as well as communal, human existences.

If it is true that the real life of philosophy consists in individuals who exchange and, to a certain extent, share their thoughts by speaking to one another, while listening, learning, teaching, varying and handing over traditions, and referring to recognized authorities, then the transcendentality of their speaking includes much more than a priori patterns of thought and language. For example, it includes the adventures of common and personal histories. We share a philosophical culture with a characteristic ethos and a whole range of standard texts and contexts. However, all sharing must first be appropriated, and appropriation generates personal rethinking, which implies reselecting or selecting otherwise and transformation. Personalization certainly privatizes but also results in new proposals and propositions: having retrieved texts and traditions, I propose a new or renewed view for your and others' consideration. What do you think about my version of a heritage with which you likewise are familiar?

Privatization implies diversity or even a dispersion of versions, but oral and written communication reestablishes the connections between individual thinkers and produces common styles, schools, fashions, and reshaped traditions, which again must be appropriated and transformed into newer versions by other individuals. From the perspective of the latter, the history of thinking is a process that incessantly repeats the sequence of acceptance, learning, appropriation, personalization, proposing, and teaching to others, who listen and learn and appropriate, and so on.

A few remarks are necessary to prevent an all-too-simplistic presentation of the thinking process indicated above. First, the relation between private and shared thought must be analyzed with more precision. Teamwork in philosophy is certainly possible, but each participant must think and re-think the entire ensemble of descriptions, questions, distinctions, arguments, and conclusions that is the result of a cooperative preparation. Neither books, nor libraries, nor super-individual ghosts, nor spirits philosophize. The opinions and ideas that are in the air or in the mentality of a certain group do not constitute a philosophy until individuals, having acquired insight and coherence within thoughtful constellations, propose their own version of those ideas in their speaking out or writing. No philosophy can be cut into pieces that are thought by separate thinkers; each thinker must embrace the whole—though not necessarily the complete detail—of its questions and strive for understanding of its entire universe. Certainly, a good motivation implies service to the community of all who desire philosophical advice, even if they cannot reproduce the totality of philosophical arguments on which such advice is based, but the difference between philosophers and amateurs does not contradict the fact that rigorous thinking is essentially all-encompassing, because it is radical, even if the full concretization of its totality remains utopian.

A consequence of the tie that binds a philosophy to one thinking individual is that each (thus personalized) philosophy dies with its thinker. Should we call this fact tragic? An entire life of learning and invention seems to disappear at the death of its author. Is the price paid for such an amount of work not too high and the profit for others too small?

To a tragic view one can oppose the following considerations. If a dead thinker's search was serious, he or she must have found some wisdom, and this has made the thinker's life as a whole more true and meaningful. Moreover, others have received incentives for their own quest of meaning and insight; if the deceased philosopher was a writer, they still may enjoy the posthumous texts that can continue to feed their souls. "Everything must be consumed" (*Alles soll verzehrt werden*) was said by the philosopher of "absolute negation" (Hegel), when he, during an excursion, treated his students to champagne. We might hear this phrase as a recipe for philosophical exhaustion. A good death may be followed by resurrection.

A second remark concerns the transformation that a philosophy undergoes by being rethought before it is transmitted to another generation. Appropriation can vary from speaking in quotes to a revolutionary personalization that seems to leave all traditions behind. Heroes of philosophy are maximally original in rejuvenating or uprooting former paradigms, while epigones accomplish the necessary task of remembering memorable pasts.

Third, when we present the thinking process as a succession of initiation, learning, appropriation, and mastery, this must be understood as a simplification of a quasi-chronological structure in which learning and mastery remain contemporary. For what else is learning to think (and to speak) than to think (and to speak) in a tentative way; and what is mastery, if it is not the ongoing attempt to discover something new, even if it is only a consequence of something that we already know? A real dialogue is the best proof of the synchronic diachrony that combines receptivity toward information with responses that transform the received information or replace it by new information (for example, by an amendment or refutation).

Fourth, the simple sequence sketched above shows how a pupil becomes a colleague who no longer follows the overwhelming guidance of other thinkers, but still depends on the exchanges that animate the philosophical debate. However, in the course of their formation, ambitious adolescents may be struck by the idea that it must be possible to escape the mutual dependence characteristic of the ongoing conversation: how can I transcend the economy of processual exchange and the *polemos* of unending differences in thought?

If it is true that thinking is done by individuals and that each of them is at the same time a historically unique and a universalizable ego, it must be possible that each historical ego embraces in its universally valid consciousness the truth of the entire universe. But then it is also possible that one ego (e.g., mine) speaks in the name of all egos and not only in her or his (e.g., my) own name. In other words, we must find access to the essence of thought as it is produced by the universal Ego that inhabits all historical egos. There is nothing wrong with this "essentialism" except, perhaps, the assumption that we are able to separate the essential and universal ego from the individual one in our words and presentations. Such a separation entails a specific conception of individual historicity and personal unicity. The latter would not make a difference, if the essential Ego speaks its mind through our historical and each time unique voices. Over against the essential universality of valid philosophy, the unicity of the existing philosopher would represent no more than existentially irrelevant instances of a silent but universally valid "voice": the silent voice of a univocal, apersonal or superpersonal but still human thought that can and must be translated into the many languages of real men and women.

Individual Thinkers and the Good

What if, however, the multivocal unicity of existing persons cannot be experienced as accidental or irrelevant with regard to the truth? What if essences are neither to be despised nor to be seen as the most radical and ultimate elements of the universe and its being? If individual lives are primarily oriented by the Good (and thus by the human desire of becoming good oneself), would the most decisive relation then not lie in the bond that ties individual unicity to the super-cosmic, super-universal, and super-essential Good to which metaphysical (and metaessential) thought has always pointed before some moderns confused the difference between the solidarity of the One with the individually unique, on one side, and the essential universality that guarantees the all-encompassing totality of every kind of universe, on the other?

If the language of habitual philosophy is bound to essential predicates and structures, the One or the Good cannot be approached without apophatic language (which, however, remains always bound to preceding and accompanying *kataphasis*). The translation of the Good's way of "not-being" into essential language is then always supported by references to essential parts and structures of the totality of all beings (which, as beings in the plural, are essentially finite), but the apophatic negations obscure the meaning of such references.[1] Although the basic movement elicited by Desire precedes and transcends all confusions without abolishing their obscurity, the Good reveals itself to our attempts at translation through multiple versions of obscured clarity. The difference that separates it from the essential universe cannot be mastered by any defining, thetic, or systematic wording. Such wording is the expression of our speaking *about*, insofar as this is thematic, panoramic, encompassing, totalizing, and thus essential. The question of whether certain forms of speaking-*to* are able to maintain and express the difference between the Good and the essences will keep us searching in the next chapter. For now it is sufficient to see (1) that the Good, as unifying orient and origin of all human motions, including those of thought, demands a trans-essential language, which the modern Cogito cannot offer, and (2) that it can be approached and even reached but not captured by a variety of clear-obscure translations for which well-oriented individuals are responsible.

In light of the Desire that drives us beyond essentiality, the philosophical endeavor is no longer a definitive mapping of the universe, but rather the search for an access to what invites us from the other side of essence. Accepting this invitation does not abolish the investigation of the universe, but (re)situates all beings and their interconnectedness—i.e., the entire economy of universal truths—in their anagogic references to the Good. Thus, they owe their essential universality and the universe owns its unicity to an orientation that can neither be possessed nor mastered because it relativizes as well their essence as the versions in which the universe is presented by the thematic views of essence-loving thinkers.

To come back to the thinkers who understand that essentiality and universality are necessary but not enough, they can no longer stop at a transcendental Ego producing universally valid theories about the universe. They must recognize the referential relativity of their own unicity as always already touched and provoked by the Good, which manifests itself in our absolute desire for the super-essential Absolute.

How must thinkers think, when this perspective of philosophy has become the horizon of their noematic commitment? Before developing the ultimate perspective of philosophy (is this expression an oxymoron?), we should return to the situation of thinking individuals in conversation with one another.

The Community of Difference

Having rediscovered that every thinker is unique without being isolated, we must ask which consequences follow from the statement that the universality of thought and the community of thinkers cannot be reduced to the coherence of a shared theory. The essences (i.e., the modes of being) of all kinds of existents cannot be separated from their referential alliance to the Good that co-determines their radical and ultimate meaning. This meaning is at stake when thinkers ask themselves and others how they should deal with all that is in the universe. Dealing with beings, while respecting their modes of existing, includes following not only the suggestions by which all phenomena guide our responses to their appearance, but also their pointing beyond themselves to the Good that makes them existentially decisive. As mediating between the Good and each individual's unique existence (with its task of existing well), all essences are permeated by the effective, practical, and theoretical modes that are typical for the individual's way of being attracted and influenced by the Good. The singularity of lived (i.e., enjoyed, endured, and performed) existence as oriented by the ultimate Desirable is the basic perspective that encompasses all the universally valid elements of shared thought. All essentiality is interpreted in as many ways as there are acting, feeling, and speaking individuals. Because "the soul is somehow all things,"[2] each interpretation is at the same time unique and all-encompassing, and therefore as well congruent with as fundamentally different from any other. Convergence and affinity, rather than identity, characterize all interpretations that approach the truth.

As a world of endless multiplicity, philosophy refers to one never-quite-captured target that fascinates without end. Each philosopher repeats the entire work of thinking about the universe as mediating between singular lives and the Good of all. Consequently, the multiplicity of basic perspectives generates not only fragments but alternative systems. The diversity of visions that follows from the multiplicity of thinkers' unicity does not abolish the task of every time again discovering the coherence of the universe, but it relativizes all philosophical universes, while relating them as individually and qualitatively different approaches of the truth within families of thought.

If thinking is no longer practiced in separation from the desire for the truth of a good life, philosophy cannot be separated from the existential quest for wisdom. Good philosophy then implies real adventures and the maturity of life's own experience. As result of a uniquely lived and thoughtful life, a personal philosophy is irreplaceable and unrepeatable. Imitation is possible, but it does not lead to authentic thought unless it is reborn into a new, personally experienced version of the admired model.

The singularity of each personalized—and in this sense original, not merely epigonal—thought presupposes and necessitates conversation. Even if an isolated ego were able to produce an exemplary interpretation of the universe, this interpretation would not play any role, if it were not offered as appropriatable to one or more recipients. These, however, cannot receive any view without transforming it into an element of their own life and thought, which are already oriented and formed in different ways. Just as any proposed theory incorporates preceding thoughts, so its listeners or readers are provoked to new retrievals.

Instead of considering the similarities and differences between philosophies in terms of universal truth and individual instantiations, we should understand the variety of historically situated and individual approaches to the truth as a multitude of approximations through which the Good presents itself in the dimension of thought.

Once we discover that the differences following from each thinker's unicity cannot be surpassed by a super-theory in which all differences are *aufgehoben* (integrated) into one overall and absolute knowledge of the absolute, we must give up the illusion of an anonymous and universally valid standpoint from which one could judge, amend, adjust, or integrate all subordinate—particular and individual—perspectives. For didactic and historical purposes, the fiction of such a super-standpoint may be useful or even necessary, but all the views and overviews that are produced from it confirm that these likewise express individualized interpretations and metainterpretations of the various philosophies they try to classify. The only honest response to philosophy's singularization lies in a more humble stance: that of a participant in the conversation. Such a participation does not exclude a certain kind of competition (shouldn't everyone try to offer the best one can in the common pursuit of truth?), but it excludes the idea that one human thought can put an end to the differences that separate all philosophies. In other words, participation and commitment exclude the possibility of one superphilosophy, while including the necessity of confrontation between divergent versions and approximations.

How has this confrontation been organized and how should it be? Speaking and writing impose their own rituals on the encounter of individualized systems, theories, views, and experiences. Mutual understanding presupposes a fund of already shared convictions, but in displaying one's own thought, one counts on the interlocutor's willingness to host, albeit briefly, those personal and personalized elements that single one's thought out as "mine." Whether the other will make use of them cannot be predicted, but a refusal of considering my thoughts as shareable—perhaps even universally—would prevent all dialogue. Competition is not the best condition for careful listening and polemics may cause even more distortion, whereas a shared dedication to nothing else than truth generates the greatest benevolence in reception and fair evaluation. Benevolence, receptivity, the art of careful listening and perceptive reading, love of truth and hatred of falsehood, justice and prudence in critical evaluation are (partly ethical, partly noetical) virtues that condition the quality (i.e., the degree of trustworthiness and closeness to truth) of a conversation. If, as we have argued, dialogue is essential for any philosophical method and epistemology, these presuppose morally no less than theoretically excellent skills.

It is not necessary to love one's interlocutor, but friendship (in the sense of mutual goodwill based on shared love for truth with all the virtues attached to it)[3] is a necessary condition. Dependent on the dispositions of the speakers, the presence of the Good in the practice of their thinking causes cooperation or combat, shared contemplation, critical evaluation, more or less friendly amendments, peaceful reception, or rejection. Ideally, the speakers are motivated by love of the Good as expressed in truth and universal well-being, but in reality this love is often mixed with many less ideal motivations. The necessary purification of our motivation demands more than theoretical consideration, because the Good transcends ideas and intelligence. First of all, it demands passion and dedication. A certain kind of "faith" or devotion is required for practicing members of the philosophical republic. As such, we share a range of convictions and rituals that have taken a specific social, ethical, cultural, and historical shape. Consequently, an insight into the conditions of truth-oriented thinking presupposes a full analysis of the social, cultural, moral, religious, political, and historical aspects of the philosophical republic insofar as they are relevant for truthful thought.

But how and where should such an analysis begin? At this point we encounter a classical aporia: how can we correctly examine the conditions of correct thinking before we know how to think correctly about anything (including those conditions)? While trying to develop a theory about the right mode of thought, preliminary thought seems unable to justify its own procedures; but how then can it justify any other thought?

In fact, we have already practiced thinking before questions about its conditions emerge: preliminary questions most often coincide with the metaquestions that follow the more naïve exercises and experiments of a more or less intuitive kind of thinking. The attempt to lay the foundations for correct procedures by way of a fully justified methodology cannot start from a *tabula rasa* or a not-yet-engaged point of departure; it proceeds by way of progressive emendation—an emendation that, though less naïve, still—at least partly—is led by intuitions rather than by demonstrations. Most of the latter come later as retrospective justifications. However, when I began to think, interventions of others gave me more guidance than original intuitions of my own, and even now my thinking is continually reawakened, corrected, widened, and enriched by others. As a philosopher I should be a good listener or reader, although too much complacency with regard to recommended authorities might block my struggle with questions that are genuinely my own.

If it is true that a thinker's goal cannot lie in a final triumph over all real or possible interpretations, integration of influences has the status of an individual experiment that—within the limits of one's own selection and skills—transforms a certain amount of borrowed insights into elements of a personal—and thus unique—synthesis, which then is offered as one possibility of thought to other seekers of the truth. The structure of an ongoing conversation—with its patterns of teaching, learning, imitation, integration, refutation, propagation, and so on—forces all participants to speak and listen or to read and write without end. When observing the movement of selection, appropriation, exchange, handing on, and communication, in which individual thinkers are caught, while also analyzing the rituals in which this movement is expressed, we may conclude that the individual essence of philosophy does not escape a shared economy and even a "market" of thought. Does this economy have an essence of its own? Is it a higher, more substantial, more dominant and relevant source of thought than the originality of thinking geniuses? Is it not rather an inseparable moment of the thinker's thinking itself, which thus manifests the relevance of the social, shared, communal dimension from which it emerges?

You and I Are Speaking

Until here, I have continued to write from the viewpoint of someone who oversees the philosophical community from the outside or from above. This meta- or super-position clearly contradicts the thrust of the descriptions I have proposed: if thinking is not alive except as personalized (and thus individual) participation in the ongoing communication of dialoguing individuals, and if such a communication entails every time a unique commitment of speakers or writers who, in their exchange, want not only to talk about the truth, but also to be in and committed to the truth, they cannot avoid presenting their thoughts in first-person language, while at the same time inviting or provoking others to respond.

One obvious manner of writing in first-person language is the letter, a literary genre that was popular in the "republic of letters" of the seventeenth and eighteenth centuries. In a similar vein some treatises of that time were addressed to potential but unknown readers by words like these: "Here, dear reader, we see that . . ." However, to the extent that letters become fictional when they are used as a literary genre, such personalizations remain anonymous. They are caught in an economy of general exchangeability.

There are other ways to personalize a text. For example, I can transform the text that you, dear reader, just have read, into a personal address if I explicitly assure you here and now that it contains the philosophical conviction to which I am committed, although I am willing to change it, if you convince me to do so. You must then read every sentence of the presented text as an abbreviation of sentences that are preceded or followed by phrases like: "I assure you that . . ."; "I am demonstrating that . . ."; "This is how I see it"; "I suggest that . . ."; and so forth. In fact, as readers, we do understand most theoretical texts in this way: as addressed by the authors to all real or potential readers—as a lesson, or as a proposal in hope of a response, or as an answer to opinions that the reader might have. In writing, I direct my words to every possible reader who understands my language and shares at least some assumptions with me. I thus also target you, my reader, even if I do not know anything else about you than that you, at a certain moment in the future, may read what I am writing here and now.

However, in writing for you *and* every other possible reader, I write to no one in particular. And, in philosophy, this makes me cautious and almost mute in revealing characteristics of my own that make me unique and unrepeatable. My commitment to you—this singular reader here and now—is thus again diluted and generalized; instead of treating you as a comrade or friend to whom I am devoted through personal attention, I hide my individuality behind the mask of an "I" that speaks to every possible, but equally indeterminate, "you." Can we, in the end, not escape the universalization of any here-and-now of you and me? Certainly, if you are my intimate friend, I can try to protect my personal message—this confident text to this unique and irreplaceable you—against anyone else's prying, but why would my private communication with you alone be relevant for philosophy? If the content is philosophical, its meaning and relevance transcend all interests that are exclusively yours and mine. At least possible "you"s are then co-intended in what I write to you. Moreover, if you do not destroy my letter, others too can read it before or after your death. Because I can foresee this possibility, I might take my precautions while writing to you, in which case the letter will have lost even more of its personalized meaning.

Speaking and Writing

At this point, the difference between speaking and writing matters. *Scripta manent*, so that they can be read by many, whereas speech reaches only the actual listeners and vanishes afterward. (Let's provisionally forget the many ways in which speech can be recorded and reproduced).

When I speak to you, my attention to you is guaranteed. Even if my desires or background thoughts distract me from the argument I am explaining, my speech may remain on target, keeping our communication within the structure of a unique face-to-face that cannot be taken over by other persons.

Addressing an audience has a more complex structure, but a fundamental element of our face-to-face relationship remains the same, although the way I can talk to you as one of you-in-the-plural is not identical with the way in which I would speak to you if you and I were alone. While I myself still may be perceived as unique, my audience shows a certain anonymity: "We are here as associates . . . , as colleagues . . . , as members of . . . , as scholars . . . , as students . . . , as citizens . . . , as believers . . . , as friends," and so on. The extremes between which we move when expressing our thoughts are a private dialogue with one unique interlocutor who captivates my whole attention, on one side, and the spatially as well as temporally unlimited audience of all who might read what I write, on the other. In speaking, however, the interlocutors are restricted to a group of spatially and temporally close persons whose speaking, listening, and responding binds them together while giving voice to philosophy as practiced in the unique situation of inter-facing participants.

Technical devices for reproducing the spoken word blur the distinction between speaking and writing; but they do not make a text radically different from musical scores, which also need reanimation by good interpreters to deliver the meaning of their script.

The rush to writing and publishing has taken abnormal proportions. In philosophy, it is favored by the standards that today are set for hiring and tenure; but how many texts play an effective role in the ongoing debates? What the well-marketed stars produce might be read (or misread) by millions, but what about the production of publications that are hardly noticed? Do the latter bear more fruit than the oral lessons through which good teachers educate the next generation of thinkers? Of some great thinkers we possess student notes and tapes, but most of the time we prefer their less spontaneous, better composed, and duly revised writings over the immediate fixations of their spontaneous speech. Yet, we would rush to their classes if we could attend them, even if their improvisations are less polished and precise than the written products on which they spent their utmost care during self-critical revisions. What do we miss in listening to the recording of great teachers and what do we experience in attending their classes? The answer is obvious: it is the active presence of thinkers who not only present us with expressions of great thoughts (which most often can also be found in their publications), but also, and in the first place, show how they tackle serious questions with a passion that is no less existential than professional, while constantly provoking their audience to join as passionately, critically, and creatively as possible their devotion to the search. Oral teaching is irreplaceable because genuine thought refuses to be separated from its source: living thinkers who do not exhaust their commitment to truth by displaying a doctrine or method through fitting sentences of a well-constructed discourse. Insofar as real thinking coincides with a life devoted to the quest for truth, no other kind of discourse can replace the outspoken presence of such a form of existence.

Textuality implies a loss of life, and writing cannot entirely overcome its posthumous character. It emphasizes human mortality by always showing features of a testament (and thus constituting a possible heritage for others who come afterward). In order to remain alive—and thus be instructive and inspiring—some presenters are always needed to reanimate the relics of a great mind, albeit in the form of simple readers who try to understand and explain what they read.

We thank living and dead thinkers for their gifts, but these cannot survive if no heirs cooperate in the renewal of their meaning. Are philosophical texts more strictly regulated than musical scores, so that the actualization of their (virtual) meaning leaves less leeway for interpreters? This is not certain at all, but if so, it still remains true that no work of art or thought makes sense unless it is re-presented—i.e., appropriated and handed on by living and thinking individuals who (re)produce it through their (re)thinking, (re)playing, (re)enacting, (re)living, and (re)enjoyment—all of which, of course, make a difference.

From Listening to Speaking in Philosophy

The title of this chapter announced a concretization of the structure and the modes that chapter 2 found in speaking and dialogue, but we were immediately seduced by the "world" that philosophers share and the kind of community that emerges from their concentration on common issues and their position with regard to their universe. It is now time for a more systematic analysis of the speaking that characterizes philosophy.

Nobody is born as a philosopher. To become one, it takes many years, during which one is drilled, formed, educated, acculturated, and normalized within the familiar, social, national, cultural, historical framework into which parents and educators initiate a child. Before philosophy begins, one has already become a young man or woman who knows and practices what one is supposed to do, know, think, appreciate, and so on as a participant in some particular culture. The transition of naïve conformity to a more or less philosophical existence begins when utterances of some philosopher awaken one's desire to not only understand but also participate in the kind of speaking that is performed. It is not necessary that the first philosopher who enters my life be critical or revolutionary (although an attack on accepted mores might help); it is enough that a specific kind of reflection and perspective appear as exciting and inviting. All philosophy begins with listening—to paying attention to someone who practices philosophy while speaking to a hearer who thereby becomes a listener.

Someone else draws my attention, awakens my mind, seduces me by presenting an amazing kind of language, which opens a new world for me—or rather a new perspective on the very world in which I already have learned to live. How can I be seduced to this new mode of speaking about the world and our life in it? If it gives me a thrill and a new sort of satisfaction, must I not be inhabited by a slumbering desire for philosophy? Whence does such a desire come? Why do I want to know more about such speaking? Is it truth—*the* truth—that attracts me, speaks to me in the philosophical pronouncements that strike me? Does the truth then not speak in other ways? If it does, what is the characteristic attraction of the philosophical way?

These are difficult questions, which, as I later will learn, also trouble the most accomplished philosophers, but at the beginning of my new adventure such questions are too difficult. For now, I just want to get acquainted with a practice that seems interesting. Let me therefore learn from those who are skilled in philosophy. Listening, ruminating, repeating, and paraphrasing what they say, and if I am smart, asking a question or two might be my first response and the beginning of my participation.

Each thinker's past initiation to philosophy is unforgettable. The transition from a naïve but already formed existence to a life that is marked by philosophy cannot be erased from later developments. In the latest work of the greatest thinkers we always find traces of their first steps in thought. In any case, the transition from naïveté to philosophy cannot be understood as a *creatio ex nihilo*. The fact that, during a relatively short period of Western history, young people have been introduced to philosophy by being told that authentic philosophy begins with a *tabula rasa* or with the almost-nothing of universal doubt, has been a lie whose stubborn impact—even on postmodern thinking—we have not yet completely overcome. As far as the history of philosophy is concerned, we must firmly conclude that no philosophy has ever been developed in faithfulness to the device of such a beginning. Descartes himself was honest enough to state that his new point of departure did not and should not change anything in the existential practice of the modern philosopher with regard to the social, religious, and moral customs of his time.[4] Neither he nor any other thinker of the entire Western history has ever created a philosophical world out of the chaos, the nothing, or the indubitable evidences that are left when we strip our world of all that can be doubted in some abstractly general way. Philosophy is no creation; it does not start from (almost-)nothing, but only from a sufficiently grown and educated—albeit naïve or primitive—life. Philosophizing emerges as a shift or variation or amendment of a pre-philosophical but grown-up life, from which it emerges as a specific use of this life in a skillful language of its own. As part of an overall practice of life, philosophy is entangled with other desires and endeavors, while emphasizing life's desire for lucidity.

The message that philosophy would emerge as a creation out of (almost-)nothing may sound as a prophetic call to liberation from all the customs and prejudices that we never wholeheartedly embraced because we never were wholly convinced of their legitimacy. Soon enough, however, we discover that the burden posed on us by universal doubt—and the tasks of rebuilding in theory the entire universe, including the foundations of our own existence—is much too heavy. Nobody is an Atlas. None of the modern philosophers has done what he or she promised to do in the name of a fully emancipated, autonomous, and autarchic science of wisdom. On the contrary, the history of old and modern philosophy proves as clearly as sunlight in a cloudless sky that every philosopher draws the core and inspiration and force of his or her thought from a fund that cannot be reduced to universal evidence and indubitable principles. Existence itself remains the primary source of all inspiration, even in philosophy.

Participation in philosophy begins when the philosophical activity of one or more speakers awakens a slumbering passion in a willing listener. Intelligence is not enough for such a disposition. Some physicists or historians might enjoy a higher IQ than good philosophers, but philosophy presupposes a specific interest and a characteristic sensibility. It is difficult to say which elements exactly foster or resist the transition from average participation in the general culture to being at home in philosophy, but one thing is certain: a fitting encounter between an actual philosopher and a future one—the *Augenblick* in which the philosophical spirit sparks over—is not possible at all if both the speaker and the listener do not share some common heritage in language, culture, interest, and appreciation. A beginner is awakened to a new way of speaking and experiencing, but its novelty would be confusing if it could not be understood as a meaningful twist of more conventional language and experience.

A certain distance from the "normal" ways of a shared culture and some shocking effects are inevitable, but a hasty adoption of impenetrable words and phrases easily results in faking rather than translation or elevation. The culture from which a new thought emerges is taken for granted as result of a historical past. It represents one or more traditions and contains the popularized sediments of past philosophies. Even if some of these still seem revolutionary for a beginner—are Marx, Nietzsche, or Freud still revolutionary?—they constitute a heritage whose transmission presupposes good education. However, participation in thinking demands more than knowledge about the theses and methods of past philosophies. History of old and recent thought certainly is a useful exercise (and all that can be offered to a beginner is already history), but everything depends on the quality of the reanimation with which teacher and pupil together here and now bring their heritage to a new life. Because thinking is always a re-thinking, conservation as well as renewal are essential elements. Unless we use the adjective "conservative" to characterize the repetitive kind of resistance to any renewal, we must recognize that all thinking is as much conservative as it is progressive. Even most revolutionary philosophies are to a great extent rediscoveries, masked translations or transformations of some past. To recognize the necessary connections between works of the past and the inauguration of a new form of thought one needs memory. Because no human memory can fathom philosophy as a whole, it is always selective, even in its collective forms. A new beginning is thus always partial.

The idea of an all-around acquaintance with philosophy is difficult to realize. Historical knowledge of its past might be attainable to a certain degree; but how can this past be converted into a thematic thought that is oriented toward truth alone? Contradictory theories force one to choose or to invent a new solution, while each original theory entails a refutation or emendation of other theories. Because the enormous task involved in a thoughtful retrieval of "the past" is too burdensome for one person, we see that currents and schools emerge, each of which has its own orthodoxy and authorities. As human (all-too-human) institutions, such schools—headed by acclaimed leaders—acquire power, thus restricting the liberty of thinking for their adherents and trying to extend their influence by political activities. The funding of fellowships for work in the preferred style, the publication of encyclopedias that present a school's orthodoxy as the most or only serious doctrine, the controlled hiring of teachers, the organization of ideologically correct congresses, and grants for further developments are a few means that are used by such powers. But, fortunately, this type of institutionalization is not almighty: great thinkers from Descartes, Spinoza, and Kant to Nietzsche, Wittgenstein, and Levinas have accomplished their revolutions without subservience to such regulations. However, it is not certain that all of them would be the best teachers for students who want to know what is going on in philosophy. Most geniuses are too much themselves to introduce beginners to the overall world of philosophy, which is not populated by geniuses alone.

The tension between ongoing "business" and creative thought is essential for all teaching in philosophy. Every philosopher is supposed to have a thought of his or her own, while at the same time teaching in a generally acceptable way what students must know if they want to be part of the philosophical community. In guiding them, a teacher cannot avoid presenting a particular perspective, selection, appreciation, and critique of authors and subjects, but she remains also responsible for a "general" overview of the discipline she teaches.[5] Even if some students are very critical, they will not be completely immune to their teacher's guidance. But is their acquaintance then not biased from the outset? However, the alternative would consist in some kind of information from which all life has disappeared. Who wants fossils instead of thoughtful lives?

Here we stumble on a fundamental problem that regards not only every introduction but also the continuation of philosophy. Although we want to acquire a complete insight in the entire field of knowledge and a non-biased, universally valid viewpoint from which such an insight is possible, we discover that we are not able to possess an entirely non-particular and non-individual, universal, and absolute knowledge. If such a knowledge were possible, it could only be expressed in a superlanguage that nobody can understand or speak or write. The search for a formalized system of signs that transcends all cultures can be interpreted as a striving for such universal and utterly neutral validity, but it is obvious that formalisms not only exclude much of the reality they would like to embrace, but also imply a particular—and to that extent biased—perspective and ontology.

The tension between sought universality and factual individualization causes the basic plurality that characterizes the world of philosophy. Each thinker who, like Hegel, wants to summarize and overcome the multiplicity of existing thoughts, constructs a new brand of (super-)philosophy, which soon will be opposed by other summaries and overcomings. The multiplicity of theories is reproduced on the level of super-theory after super-theory.

With regard to the meaning of the (old and recent) past without which there is no heritage and consequently no possibility of initiation, the normal reaction of a student is a mixture of passion, curiosity, surprise, emulation, and gratitude, in various proportions according to the quality of teacher and student. While gratitude looks back, discovering and emulation open a hopeful future. Thus, the time of learning is structured as a time of acknowledged dependence on a bequest and the emerging of a new configuration. The bequest is experienced as an incompletely fulfilled promise, whereas the future is accepted as a de-constructive transformation that retrospectively changes the meaning of the heritage. What deserves gratitude most of all is not the much-needed gift of clearly explained theories, judiciously selected texts, well-conducted tests, and helpful corrections of assignments, but rather the challenging presence of instructors who are doubly devoted to their students and the sake of truth.

Why does the voice of a teacher deserve gratitude? Because no text or issue or device would reach anybody if it were not directed, addressed, said, and "dedicated" by a living person to a listener, who thereby is affected, touched, awakened, surprised, challenged, and demanded to respond. Texts, treatises, questions, and answers rest, as relics and scores, in museums and libraries, but thinking is learned by being exposed to speaking and the necessity of responding. Speaking is the most proper element of philosophy; all other forms of communication—among them writing—are subordinate tools or surrogates.

The importance of speaking does not lie solely in its indispensable use for the revival of texts. Truth itself needs living voices to affect us. I hinted at this when I asked what would be so special in attending classes given by great thinkers: there is something in their speech that gets lost when it is written or inscribed. An entire person is involved in a voice that addresses me if it is true that thinking involves the existence of a human individual—encompassing, for example, his passions, moods, heart, experiences, and adventures, much of which is lost when the presentation of such thinking is reduced to a text or video.

The panoramic view of the modern Cogito—with its super-personal (i.e., impersonal) egocentrism—isolates itself in order to enjoy a universal perspective. However, it would be too silent to be perceived if it did not subordinate itself to speakers or writers who, as you and me, communicate in a particular language and an individual style, while referring to geographically and historically contingent adventures. All of these contain general elements, but these cannot be extracted from them as their full but hidden truth. Instead, the abstracted elements only offer an abstract schema—not even a real skeleton—of the endlessly varied thinking that is never done by a universal ego or a superindividual god, but only by persons who listen and respond to one another because they have discovered that their differences imply enough affinity to make them colleagues in a shared pursuit of at least some wisdom.

Their universe is not primarily composed by all the galaxies of an expanding cosmos or the many periods of history, although a vague awareness of these dimensions is not excluded from their discussions. Their "all" is all that matters for the "real thing" and "the ultimate" that can and should and does make their and all others' existences meaningful. Their communication keeps them together in a philosophical kind of friendship and their questions are colored by their situation, although they reach out to humanity by opening themselves to the questions and debates that are going on in other communities of thought.

In abandoning the panoramic mastery of modern philosophy, you and I do not stop thinking about "all things" and their whole. Philosophical friendship does not destroy universality, but changes its meaning. The impetus that moves our thinking unavoidably extends to the ultimate horizon of allness, but whatever you or I discover within this horizon is presented and offered to you or me by particular others who talk to us or wrote for us. No thinker can stop at a part of the universe. We always want to comprehend existence as such, the world as a whole, the truth of the entire space-time in which we dwell; but life itself teaches us concentration and self-limitation. In handing over to me what you think (which always includes your perspective on the human universe), you appeal to my universe as open to the view that you pro-pose to me. Your proposition always conveys a direct or indirect, explicit or implicit view of the world as a whole, while my response confronts you with my world as crystallized in another proposition. Our communication is an encounter of worlds, even if we do not pay attention to the big questions of totality, being, or universality.

While listening to gifted teachers, a beginning student experiences his initiation as a challenge. The version of philosophy that is offered might awaken the student's admiration, which naturally issues in repetition and paraphrasing. Once acquainted with the specific bent and language practiced in the specific version that is thought, a pupil begins to imitate its style, thus prolonging a certain philosophical tradition. However, all traditions demand to be renewed by fresh insights and re-beginnings thanks to "original" thinkers. Therefore a good teacher stimulates her students to take a distance from her own version of the heritage and to invent intelligent forms of critique or serious—not cheap—objections. After—not before—the appropriation of the best legacies (encompassing the considerable efforts of tentative identification) comes the work of critical self-discovery and the struggle of developing a stance and manner of one's own. The transition between reverential appropriation and self-confident originality takes time—it may even take a whole life because it involves us in a debate with an unmanageable multitude of versions, interpretations, objections, debates, defenses, amendments, renaissances, and mutations. However, a nascent originality in the form of an intuition or unclear but promising feeling may express itself early, albeit clumsily and confusedly. Very good teachers are capable of fostering such seeds of renewal. Their reward consists in having assisted students who soon will become admirable colleagues or—even better—inaugural thinkers of a new period in philosophy. To be surpassed by one's pupils is the best result a teacher can wish, but even if good teaching does not produce a revolution, it has its own irreplaceable necessity in the continuation of a philosophical civilization that always is threatened by death and oblivion.

Dialogue

When pupils become colleagues, they develop their own ideas and language, but the sharing of a common past continues to support mutual understanding. An exchange between colleagues presupposes a common terminology, references to well-known traditions, and affinity in interest and questions, although their convictions and theories may differ considerably. Total agreement is neither guaranteed nor desirable: how boring and irrelevant would a perfect unisono be!

It is, however, not immediately clear how radical the differences between interlocutors might be lest they ruin all discussions from the onset. The plurality of fundamentally divergent philosophies, even within Western civilization, still causes a host of misunderstandings, and if philosophy is a practice that radically marks the philosopher's existence, we may expect that any fruitful discussion between committed thinkers begins with a mutual attempt to get acquainted with the main assumptions and the overall mindset of one's interlocutors. Since a debate between two or more embodiments of narcissism might not lead to anything new—Narcissus invites eulogies and interviews, not discussions—a philosophical conversation demands several social virtues besides the dianoetical ones that are obvious.

It is not enough—it is not even necessary—that each speaker receive as much time and attention as any other and it is an obvious falsification of the facts to presuppose that all interventions have the same weight and should be counted as equal votes. It is, however, indispensable that the participants listen to one another with sympathy and benevolence. If it is true that all speech, and especially the philosophical one, emerges from a source that lies deeper than the clear ideas of explicit reflection, the affective and as yet unconceptualized experiences behind and underneath our sentences must get a chance to be heard, even if they are expressed indirectly. The essential equality of all persons cannot be translated into equality of philosophical standing. Some philosophers are better educated, less lazy, more fortunate in their readings and encounters, and more inspired than others. If their interlocutors are wise enough, they will allot them more and better parts of the precious time than to less gifted thinkers. Democracy has very little to do with quality, especially in philosophy.

However, who is wise enough to measure the quality of philosophers? If we do not want to follow the opinion of a democratic majority, which convictions or opinions could then answer the question of who deserve our special attention? That the average majority and the fame it promotes deserve suspicion has been well known since Plato's critique of the sophists, but what right do we have to posture as members of an elite that has the monopoly of good taste and judgment?

Socrates and Plato themselves started from common opinions, but their pointed questions awakened the seed of truth that lay sleeping in the caves of a deeper self. The resurrection of "forgotten" truth occurred through the *Aha-Erlebnis* of a recognition that for the first time "saw" and felt what always already had been pre-sensed and pre-known. Both Plato and Aristotle developed a method for the transition from superficial *doxai* to deeper levels of knowing, and anamnesis—the explicitation of a priori presentiment—remained a paradigm for philosophical method and truth, at least until Hegel and Heidegger.

Does this reminder contain an answer to the question of a wise arrangement of discussions? The truth of good judgment about philosophical quality must prove itself through more than formal coherence: it must convince those (the *phronimoi*) who recognize that judgment as coming from the depth of our being one with the universe, in being oriented toward the truth. But at the beginning of a conversation such a judgment can be presented only as an opinion, albeit one that sounds familiar to philosophers that have practiced seriously for many years. It is in the discussion itself that opinions may gradually or suddenly transform themselves into trustworthy insights, even if ulterior amendments remain possible. Consequently, to enter into the conversation is to take risks: the convictions with which the exchange begins are provisional positions that must be tested by cross-examinations of their strength or weakness and their need of emendation. It remains true, however, that formal logic and empiricist evidence are not sufficient to reach a final decision about the truth of those positions and their adherents. The quality of their roots and the source from which they emerge must be sensed as promising with regard to the truth.

Concerning the interlocutors' quality, we must conclude that, at the beginning of a philosophical conversation, we can neither presuppose that all the participants are equally good at philosophy, nor give more weight and speaking time to some than to others. However, it is rare that we begin a conversation: most of the time we have already heard or read some work by or about our interlocutors and thus continue the conversation that is already going on in our mind.

One aspect of our equality in the conversation—an aspect that at the same time constitutes our inequality (and we will see that it is much more than an aspect)—consists in the fact that each of us is "I" for ourself and "You" for all others. This "aspect" is crucial but neglected or suppressed in all theories that identify the subject of philosophy either as the lonely ego of a thinking hermit or as the universal "I" that inhabits all philosophers—or as a combination of both.

Singularization of the Truth

As we have seen in chapter 1, modern philosophers preferred treatises over commentaries and disputations. Most of them considered the writing of dialogues a didactically useful and sometimes entertaining means of teaching insights that are explained more adequately in systematic monologues. These, however, had to bypass all experiences and thoughts that could not be recognized by intelligent readers. For even if an author lets himself be known, the content and form of a good treatise should be universally valid and to that extent anonymous, non-subjective, and independent of strictly individual or exceptional sources. Since experience and thought presuppose an individual subject, the basic question concerned being an individual, singularly existing, autonomous subject whose *cogito* could be recognized by all other subjects as identical with their own *cogito*. Each ego was philosophical insofar as it was a universalizable *cogito*, thinking the entire universe in a universally valid manner. The transcendental ego that inhabited, while ruling, the thinking of each existent philosopher was thematized differently, but even if it was seen as a substance, a subject, a spirit, or God, this interpretation did not change the mononoetic character of the individual thinkers' theories. Others—he, she, they, or you—were no essential parts of any *cogito*, except as material objects for the lonely thinker who gathered all individuals in a social philosophy.

Certainly the historical and educational necessity of other subjects of experience and thought cannot be denied, even by Cartesian thinkers, but their role was seen as provisional: in the end, a thorough philosopher would be able to demonstrate on his own what he had discovered, and the treatise in which he reported this would encompass everything that a reader needed to prove its truth from A to Z. Traditions and other authorities should be checked and all listening had to be replaced with the self-certainty of a magisterial deduction. In philosophy, others could function only as a detour from heteronomous thought to autonomy. Learning, advice, commentaries, conversations, and dialogues could not be more than overtures or preludes to philosophy proper.

What if, however, thinking essentially and necessarily is an endless dialogue? For example, because the unsurpassable difference between individual thinkers is so radical and all-permeating that it modifies the truth of each individual's discovery?

This is indeed a first line of argumentation for the relevance of otherness, difference, and plurality in philosophy. If each thinker is a singular subject whose historical existence is radically different from all others, and if each one's singular unicity or haecceity permeates and colors each one's approach and view of the truth, no concrete philosophy can be considered equivalent to the truth, because it is only one perspective on it. Perspectivism does not exclude that different philosophies are close to the truth, but it implies a certain degree of relativism. One can try to overcome this by gathering the best approximations—the classics—in a sort of synthesis, but such a synthesis is again the result of an individual (meta-)interpretation of that plurality. Each history or genealogy of the many perspectives and approaches implies a metaphilosophy (e.g., a Hegelian, Comtian, or Heideggerian one), which again represents a singular and different perspective on the philosophical plurality.

One could also venture the hypothesis that the irreducible differences between well-thought philosophies need not force us to a choice between them or to their *Aufhebung* in a higher synthesis. If the truth is too deep to be captured by propositions and syllogisms, a plurality of conflicting theories without a final super-theory might still be the best humanity can offer on its journey to the truth. If so, traveling with the best philosophers, despite their differences, would still be a very good manner of being on the way to truth. The fullest possible truth would then consist in a thoughtful rethinking of great philosophies, which might lead to adding a new, again approximative philosophy to their ensemble.

Even if one does not "have" or "possess" a philosophy of one's own, it is possible to come closer to the truth by (re-)thinking with the greatest thinkers of history what they, in their circumstances and times, experienced and thought about issues that, essentially or radically, are still the same. We can become wiser without strict adherence to any theory. Apparently, wisdom is something different and deeper than any theory. But then also is the desire and friendship that relates us to wisdom. Indeed, the truth does reveal itself not only—not even mainly—in the theorems of philosophy, but rather in its climate, its style, its "music," the purity or impurity of its desire and motivation, the authenticity of its stance and movement, the radicalism of its deepest—and therefore hardly self-conscious—commitment. These are the experiential qualities that solicit our sympathies and trust more radically than their empirical and logical consistency. Trustworthiness cannot be reduced to provability; it demands the emergence of a certain affinity that is undergone and lived rather than thought: a sort of faith.[6]

To be "close to" or "in" the truth differs from conceptual agreement with a true and rigorously demonstrated discourse. It is sensed in the experience of existence itself. To become good at this sensing is to become "musical," a *mousikos*, as Plato emphasized.[7] But if the surrounding culture is bad, we can only hope that "nature" (*physis*) and a "godly lot" (*theia moira*) shelter some exceptional seekers from being seduced by the lies upon which the sophists thrive.[8]

The last line of argument indicated here still represents a view "from above" upon the philosophical conversation that unites different individuals into a family of fellow travelers toward truth. However, as we argued above, by giving in to the tendency of monopolizing the historical conversation by looking down on it from an imaginary top (which then is identified as "the I"), we ruin the exchange (the *Auseinandersetzung*) and risk falling back on the modern monologue. In any case, the view from above must be subordinated to the exchange involving you and me as partners who are committed to one another (e.g., as you, the reader of these lines, to me, their writer) and who cannot melt into one supervisor who observes and comprehends what you and I are thinking while talking to one another.

You

When you and I speak to one another, we continue conversations that have occurred before, though not necessarily between you and me. Even at our first encounter, I situate you within a context, while presuming that you speak out of a certain past and might defend one of the positions I am familiar with. The same is true of your perception of me. Each conversation we will have is an opportunity to adjust our prejudices about each other, but full acquaintance and mutual understanding take perspicacity and time. Since patience and perspicacity are rare, many misunderstandings are caused by my identifying you with a picture that I have formed by amalgamating your real self with my assumptions about your sharing certain convictions and preferences of the surrounding culture. While responding and reacting to you, I then respond to that picture, which in fact might do an injustice to the person you really are.

It remains true, even in your most genuine being yourself, that you are also a representative of the culture in which you have been educated, even if your originality always—at least to some extent—transforms its ethos into a brand of your own. And, of course, you are, like all other possible yous, as human as I. Thus, you are (1) human, like all other individuals, being a subject of equal rights, (2) representative of a particular culture, and (3) an original individual with a position and style of your own. And this is true of all human individuals. Consequently, it does not define what makes this unique and unrepeatable you. From the perspective summarized here in three points, you are just an instantiation of the universal concept "human individual."

One of Kant's best thoughts about ethics is expressed in a way that seems, and perhaps is, awkward: a human person is a *Zweck an sich*, "an end in itself;" or negatively: no human individual can be reduced to being a means for anything else. A person is the end of many teleological sequences, but it is itself not a mere link or transitory stage within such a sequence. Or in Aristotelian terms: a person is that for the sake of which (*hou heneka*) one acts, desires, lives, etc., while itself cannot be defined as being for the sake of something else. If we "use" someone's works or words, we do not use that person as such, but only something *of* that person, something that he or she can lend us or permit us to use without losing precisely that which makes them persons. As an "end in (or by) itself," each person is irreducible to mediating relations; its mode of existence (its "essence") and the core of its worth do not depend on anything else than being what it (he or she as a person) is; he or she is not anything relative, but *absolute*.

How did Kant show that his thesis was true? He claims that the just quoted formulation (the second formula) of the categorical imperative follows from and fundamentally coincides with the first formula, which insists on the universability of our maxims for action.[9]

Today, though doubtful about this identity, we are inclined to endorse the second formula with more ease than the first; but for Kant, the universal (and objective, as well as necessary) character of the moral law is the radical and supreme expression of human rationality, which fills Kant with awe and founds his entire philosophy: we must respect *die Menschheit*, the humanness, in all individuals, because of its *reasonality* (*Vernünftigkeit*).

For us, the universality of reason has lost much of its supreme and radical character, although no philosopher can deny the validity of its demands. However, the absoluteness of a human individual cannot be deduced from its universality, but only from some x that precedes that universality and expresses itself in it. Kant himself hints at this, when he approaches the "final" core of a person through another access than the distinction between means and ends or between universality and individuality. From the perspective of worth, he states that human beings do not have a value, because values can be compared with one another, and thus are relative, whereas human dignity (*Würde*) transcends the totality of all values.[10] Beyond values and means, but also beyond universal laws (which are the same for all instantiations), dignity commands.

The three modes of "you" indicated above present "you" as a name for everyone who I, the one who is writing here, am not. Am I the only one who does not belong to the totality of yous that I am addressing here? Does my writing or speaking locate me outside of their gathering? Or above it? While talking about all addressable persons in a nation, a culture, a community, or humanity as a whole, social philosophers have gathered and structured the interaction of persons and communities from the summit of their egological perspective. They knew that their egos also belonged to the human society, but as philosophers they had to make a distinction between their thinking ego, which performed the overview, and their social ego, which was one among the many instantiations of the human race.

In all his work, Hegel has emphasized that universality is an abstraction of the reality (or "actuality," *Wirklichkeit*) in which it has become "concrete" (grown together) by particularization (or specification) and singularization. Individuals are the being-real and the being determined or "being-there" (*Dasein*) of all universality.[11] At the same time, Hegel has insisted on the impossibility of talking sensibly about any individual here and now without immediately presenting it as instance of a universal essence or concept. Thinking, according to Hegel, cannot escape universalization; in philosophy, one cannot grasp any "you" without including all other possible addressees.

However, philosophers incessantly address other singular and irreplaceable philosophers, at least implicitly, when they criticize others' theories or defend their own against Kant, Hegel, Nietzsche, Heidegger, or contemporary thinkers of note. Often such names stand for theories that have become trends or schools, but polemics and conversation from one to one remain a reality. Apparently, individuals can isolate and target this one other individual here and now without immediately immersing that thinker in the universality of all others. Addressing someone is radically different from grasping or thematizing or talking *about* that person.

The bird's-eye view of an ego that views the universe must be overcome in order to address someone as this unrepeatable, non-universalizable, unique you, of which there is only one in the world and its history. Addressing transcends the universe.

As soon as I realize that participation in philosophy not only involves me in talking about the universe or some topic within its boundaries, but also, and primarily, in a face-to-face relationship with people to whom I speak, my understanding of the philosophical "game" changes radically. No longer can I perceive myself exclusively as a thinking ego to whose inspection all beings offer themselves as components of an unlimited natural, social, and historical universe. For this perspective—if possible at all—can only be a subordinate element of my conversation with particular individuals to whom my thinking is directed.

The Audience

What can we say about the philosopher's audience? To begin with, we must state and restate that nobody can claim the standpoint that Archimedes wished to have in order to master (and then to possess or even to reconstruct and re-create) the universe. The wish to be the god of the universe, at least in thought, may be seen as the summit of narcissism because it excludes all otherness. We do not overcome it by endless talking and writing *about* otherness, difference, impossible unity, violence, or transgression, but only by really or "existentially" descending from the summit to the lowlands of a thoughtful conversation in which I perform and experience the radical difference between *you* (in the singular or the plural) and *me* (who here and now listens and responds to you) as *basic* (without pretending that I can sublate the full truth of that difference into a synthesis of my own).

Before we attempt to determine the proper structure of this difference, let us ask who are the speakers and listeners on whom we count when speaking or writing in philosophy.

It might be a dream of adolescents and the powerful to imagine that their words should be heard by all people. The contemporary media system may thrive on such a dream, but a grain of realism suffices to understand that even the Bible, Plato, and Shakespeare cannot be received everywhere until universal education has fundamentally transformed the entire humanity. Many holy books are meant to be read or paraphrased in all languages and nations. This is natural insofar as they are supported by the conviction that they reveal the ultimate and overall meaning of being human. Can philosophical writings express a comparable claim?

Ordinarily philosophers speak to students, colleagues, or amateurs, but through writings and electronic devices they can reach out to a wider audience, most of whose reactions remain invisible and inaudible. Some thinkers may feel that they must address humanity as a whole or even its posterity, but this kind of universality remains an illusion, though its abstract possibility is implied in the unlimited character of thought. But how could one person or school speak in the name of a universal truth that manifests itself in a thousand languages, cultures, and histories?

A more realistic self-conception confronts the philosopher with an immediate audience whose assumptions and expectations are more or less known to her, so that she does not need to begin at the very beginning, but can connect with the sedimentations of many traditions, lessons, writings, and conversations from which this audience here and now has profited. Can we typify the interaction—the play of speaking and responding—between a philosopher and his listeners? To answer this question, we cannot ignore the kind of speaking and listening at which the two parties aim. If I want to impress my listeners in the hope of attracting their admiration for my knowledge or rhetorical skills, I am not really interested in their responses, except insofar as these express or imply praise or fame. I am not even interested in their love of knowledge or wisdom, because my own love has replaced these with my own "admirable" and attention-hungry self.

If I have not lost or betrayed my friendship with wisdom, I may want to tell what has become obvious—at least to me—in the common search for truth, while inviting my listeners to a critical response. It is also possible that I am so convinced of an insight or theory that I do not count on discussion but only desire attentive listening, in the hope that my audience will profit from the long and arduous work that has resulted in relevant knowledge. In this case, I am more inclined to take questions than to make myself vulnerable by challenges to contention. Then, I approach, and consequently perceive, my audience not primarily as a diversified multitude of individuals, each of whom have their own strictly personal way and story of searching for truth, but rather as a human mass that I want to convince, confirm, initiate, or convert. In the former case, when I genuinely want others to respond in their own truth-loving way, I aim at the goal of their and my becoming wiser, and I count on their desire of the same. This is the normal setting for a conversation among colleagues, but it also fits a class, when I combine initiation with challenges that demand response. Still, it is possible to withdraw, in such a setting, from a personal relationship that gives every listener an opportunity to express a strictly personal quest for philosophical wisdom. A class does not, in general, allow for the structure of you-and-i-and-you or i-and-you-and-me.[12]

Your uniqueness is approached and spoken to as unique, if my private encounter with you is inspired by the twofold virtue of friendship with truth and concern for you. A small seminar offers a better setting for such a relationship than a class, but even a seminar rarely realizes a network of such you-and-i-and-you relationships. Not only the facticity of spatial proximity, visibility, and number of listeners and speakers defines the meaning of speaking and addressing; the purposes at which the participants aim are even more essential. In focusing on my teaching, I offer my philosophizing to a limited number of interlocutors. Since my words are here and now directed only to these—let's say thirty—students, they should be useful for their endeavor to become good philosophers. This presupposes that my explanations can be understood. I must therefore know what these students already know and do not yet know, and I must replace their ignorance with acquaintance in order to foster their advancement—which all presupposes knowledge or a guess about their future. It is not necessary—it is a waste of time for them—that I engage in learned considerations or polemics without relevance to their intellectual growth. Consequently, the scope of my speaking and the horizon of my philosophical practice, insofar as this is tied to teaching, is rather limited.

Research and writing in philosophy expose me to a wider audience. In principle, I write for innumerable receivers whose assumptions are not easily determined. To get a picture of those who might read what I write, I must find out those who not only are interested in the topics I treat, but are also capable of understanding the language used, the implicit references and assumptions, and so on. If I write in Dutch, I restrict my audience to a small group of readers, even if the Dutch might read proportionally more books than members of some other countries. If I write in English, I reach out to a broader public, but will they be philosophically minded? Linguistic provincialism is one of the important factors that limit the horizon of all publications, including philosophical ones. In the United States, for example, many students and even some professors identify the secondary literature on Plato, Spinoza, Kant, or Hegel with the ensemble of publications written in or translated into English. Such a lie might be welcome to certain students, but it greatly devaluates the quality of serious scholarship.

Another factor that restricts the possible audience of a publication lies in the style and affiliation to which it testifies. Because the philosophical panorama of our time is scattered into several schools of philosophizing, often separated by a combination of ignorance and hostility, it is difficult to find studies that do not show affiliation or similarity with one style that is loathed by others. Few adherents of other schools read such studies, so that the various schools, unaware of serious challenges, risk becoming ghettos with a special brand of dogmatic partiality.

Any writer who has a realistic picture of the situation in which we today pursue the noble endeavor of thinking will take all such restrictions into account. But if we write only for a small group of possible listeners, does not the meaning of "universality"—the shibboleth of modern philosophy—change its meaning?

When I speak to actually present listeners in a dialogue or a class, I do not address humanity, but these persons here and now with whom I share a language, a particular culture, a social milieu, and many ethical assumptions. My speech is successful if it communicates philosophical elements that can be integrated by my listeners into their ongoing life. The more familiar I am with their mindset and knowledge, the better I will be able to offer them what seems to me relevant for maturing in thought and praxis. As a philosopher, I certainly will have to confront them with questions about humanity as a whole, even with the entire universe, and about the universal validity of certain insights in contrast with the particularity and the relativity of opinions that may be right for certain circumstances or cultures. However, by interacting with my class, I do not address a whole nation or culture or continent or all the religions of the world, and I would fail my task as a teacher if, there and then, I imagined myself to be addressing the whole of humanity.

Some writers have indeed become teachers for a nation, a civilization, or a worldwide religion; with some exaggeration we can call them teachers of humanity, but they became such only posthumously. However, authors who would explicitly dedicate their writings to humanity as a whole seem odd: do they really think of themselves as voices that should be listened to by all? Wouldn't that be the summit of arrogance? Yet, the *cogito* of a modern philosopher seems to speak in the name of all to every other *cogito*, i.e., to all who have a mind, without exception. Does such a *cogito* make itself necessarily the center of the universe? Does philosophical writing—in contrast with oral addresses or letters—imply the temptation of considering itself all-important and to be heard by all? Are philosophers inescapably presumptuous? Or can they and should they be universal servants, seeing their inspiration and knowledge as a gift that they—in grateful humility—must offer to anybody who wants it? Or is the very thought of oneself as being a humble servant of humanity already arrogant? Perhaps one can think of such an attitude only as a normative but never fully realized ideal.

Attempts to address all humans might be more than any individual can perform. Does it not presuppose that one speaks all languages and understands all cultures, religions, philosophies, and—at least in a sketchy mode—the lives of all real and possible individuals? If some persons posthumously become heroes of thought for many continents—for example, Saint Paul, the writers of the gospels, Plato, Kant, Marx, or Nietzsche—would their words not be interpreted in very different ways? Certainly, but this does not exclude a fundamental affinity among the admirers of those heroes. However, the initiations and discussions without which no adherence at all is possible demand regional and local teachers who speak and listen to real individuals, without setting aside the differences that are occasioned by great sources of other times and places.

If I, as a philosopher, do not have to speak in the name of all to all, but only, as this limited guardian of a limited heritage, to a particular audience here and now, I still speak to the universally human in each individual or group, but I must begin by accepting the limits of their and my own particularity, which is a mixture of universalizable convictions and individual, possibly false or shaky opinions. One, though not the ultimate or most radical, task of a philosopher consists in sorting out the elements of such a mixture, while asking how they, together, form a coherent or incoherent constellation. Much factual philosophy stops at this goal. One can take a certain constellation of opinions for granted—for example, a conviction that is popular among well-educated Americans—in order to ask whether it is coherent and how it should be expressed in scholarly terms, propositions, and theories. For instance: Are the underlying assumptions of the American ethos concerning individual freedom, human rights, and democracy correct? However, a more radical question, which philosophy cannot suppress, asks whether the overt or hidden assumptions of such a widespread ethos can be justified, but this question is not often asked and less often answered satisfactorily. The more radical question leads from the particular and still naïve framework within which a first stage of reflection and analysis is performed to deeper questions that regard all human individuals, but the thinkers' standpoints can still dogmatically stick to a typically American outlook on the whole of humanity. A discussion among such thinkers is then dominated by a characteristic agreement on the three assumptions just mentioned (and some others as well), even if the discussants sincerely wish to be open to the different assumptions of other communities and individuals. Pluralism, yes; but—of course—in American English!

Proximity and Distance

If a thinker neither possesses a freestanding and all-encompassing viewpoint from which he can observe the human universe, nor is able to address all humans of the present and the future, what remains then of the universality of a content that you and I and all other philosophers should discover and display? Even if we concede that the most radical questions and answers regard all individuals and communities of human history, should we not focus on those persons that are "near" and closely connected with us through common interests and a strong similarity in ethos or conceptions? Of course, nearness cannot be reduced to geometrical or geographical distances; some philosophers in Europe or Japan might be close to me because we pursue a common research project, and in my thinking and striving I may be closer to Saint Bonaventura than to Derrida. But can we develop a general theory about the relations between proximity and universality, beginning with some principles about the topics that are at stake: (1) the relevance of distance and nearness for our dialogues, (2) the distinction of their various levels, and (3) the impact nearness should be allowed to have on our striving for universal validity?

As already hinted above, it seems normal and defendable to begin a discussion by concentrating on the factual agreements and disagreements that characterize our exchange as expression of a culture that we share despite some disagreements. The latter might alert us to more fundamental inconsistencies in our culture, which then force us to take a distance from its obviousness in order to dig deeper into questions about the justifiability of its deepest convictions and its contrasts with other cultures based on different assumptions. Whether we will be able to discuss such questions with representatives of profoundly different cultures depends on our language skills and our empathy with regard to foreign modes of life and thinking. In surpassing the American horizon, we exile ourselves to the existence of foreigners who might be perceived as partly guests, partly strangers, or even as rootless nomads. There is no universal language in which we can speak, but familiarity with the others' language might enable us to get a sense of the "spirit" that inspires their customs and mentality.

At this moment, only a small minority of philosophers seems to be engaged in intercultural discussions that allow all the participants to express themselves in their own most genuine mode of existing and speaking without passing through the betrayal of translations into a particular language that remains foreign to them. Most often we content ourselves with an English-speaking or -writing perspective on other cultures with which we find ourselves confronted. The universality that belongs to translations of foreign cultures into English overviews is filtered through the semantic and syntactic characteristics of a particular civilization. Insofar as those cultures remain uncommon, they either remain foreign, somewhat threatening, at best hospitably respected, or they are assimilated to ethnic varieties of English patterns. In any case, it is a dream to imagine that we one day will be able to fully understand and sympathetically appropriate all the different cultures that keep humanity divided. However, the miraculous realization of such a dream does not seem necessary for the realization of a truly universal respect for all *people* in general and in philosophy.

You and I

In a conversation between you and me, one form of universality is always present: my interlocutor is always "you," this unique person with his or her uniquely personal properties, circumstances, stories, and style of life, who here and now speaks and listens to me, while I myself am likewise such a unique person, who is "you" for you. Both you and I are thus at the same time radically different (differently unique) and *the same*. The different sameness that radically separates and identifies you and me does neither coincide with the relation (or difference) between the sameness of the natural and cultural features we share, nor with the individual differences that characterize you and me as distinct instantiations of one genus "human being." Neither you nor I can be defined as a particular singularization of any universal. What "makes" you *you* and me *me* escapes any Porphyrian or other classification. All attempts to range you or me (or her or him) as instances, parts, or moments of a whole fail, because they reduce the unicity expressed in the personal pronouns "you," "he," "she," and "me" to features of a universality that effaces the radical uniquenesses of our equality-in-radical-difference.

Sciences and traditional philosophy are obsessed by generalization and identification, because their stance (the all-encompassing perspective of the onlooker) does not allow for a *looking-up to the other* that radically differs from the perspective that looks from above at all the kinds and instantiations of a gathering "con-cept" or category. The look from above necessarily looks down, thus overlooking the multiple (but neither generic, nor particularized, nor singularized) unicities of you, her, him, and me. Insofar as each of us necessarily and involuntarily escapes reduction to being a part or moment or link or function within an overall economy—i.e., insofar as each one resists all generalizing, scientific, or rational statements and theories—you and he and she and i are unrepeatable, non-interchangeable, strictly personal individuals, whose existences precede and surpass all inductions to and deductions from anything else.

The solitude that follows from each one's unicity does not isolate, however. On the contrary, it conditions the possibility of looking up to one another, of respecting you as irreducible and irreplaceable, of observing the distance that forbids any swallowing or melting together, and of discovering how uniquely super-interesting and "special" you are. Thanks to your and my uniqueness, our solitudes urge us to speak and respond (instead of devouring, exploiting, or using one another—which are the ways suggested by all forms of "economy"). Thus you and i allow for your and my being a self that deserves and claims to be approached and greeted as nothing in particular, i.e., as irreducible, irreplaceable, non-placeable at all, wholly non-relative or absolute, absolutely unique, uniquely absolute.

However, the preceding sentences are still written from a universalizing perspective. This makes them contradictory insofar as they seem to universalize the unicity about which they deny that it is a universal essence. But is there another way to respect each one's uniqueness in language—or even in living? If so, is their also another way in philosophy? Or is it the philosophers' fate that their addiction to universality causes them to betray personal unicities? But then we should ask whether such an addiction is natural and necessary or a deviation that can be cured.

I respect your unicity when my listening or speaking to you expresses respect, regard, awe—perhaps even a kind of love—for the absoluteness in you that cannot be reduced to any feature or action or function or "value" of whatever totality or universe. Such listening or speaking or looking or behaving can be translated into expressions such as the following: "The world is yours." "After you." "Here I am for you."

Such a respect is possible only if I stop placing you within the horizon of my panoramic standpoint. Only in turning toward you and addressing you do I single you out as this unique and irreplaceable center of your own world. Talking *about* you—even if it affirms and elaborates your being unique—will never do enough justice to the truth of what it tries to proclaim; only talking *to* you in a respectful mode responds adequately to that truth. It is a special mode of my *turning toward you* that liberates all my dealings with you from their tendency to subject you to my views and interests; only through such a direction can looking, well-wishing, supporting, and sympathy express my dedication. Talking about you can therefore be redeemed by addressing this talk to you, for example in a conversation with you about your health or your projects.

Of course, turning to you can also express fear, hostility, hatred, or murderous desires, but both hatred and love and whatever other mode of facing you affirm or confirm by enactment the truth that your non-universalizable uniqueness precedes and transcends your essence and all the features that characterize you as one out of many.

What does this radical difference mean for philosophy as a dialogical form of life? In the first place it implies that the uniqueness of your life should not be forgotten or diluted when you and I are discussing problems. While subordinating all themes and theses to the offering gesture of my talking *to* you and looking up to you, I also may talk *about* your and my and each other's interests, but in the end, the question of your unique destiny and destination can be neither silenced nor delayed forever. The utmost seriousness of philosophy lies in its concern for this and that person's ultimate meaning—which, in the end and from the beginning, is found in the lived life of those who abandon themselves to that "game." If we can play this game with the reckless spontaneity of a child instead of breaking down, like camels, under burdens that are too heavy, so much the better; but even Nietzsche cannot deny that a unique destiny demands the utmost attention.[13]

If the unique destiny of each singular "you" with whom I deal polarizes my dialogues, this polarization has considerable consequences for the topics and questions you and I will be discussing. To what extent does it make sense that we want or feel obliged to dedicate our philosophizing to "universal" questions or interests? Are we interested in, should we really be interested in the question of whether there is life on Mars? What is, for human existence, the relevance of an encompassing theory about the origin of galaxies? Should we not restrict our discussions to those questions whose importance for each real you that concerns me here and now (and thus also for me) can be shown or surmised?

More than the content, however, it is the mode of our communicating with one another that is at stake. If my speaking and writing about things is dominated by a dedication that commands me to offer my thoughts as contributions to the realization of your destiny, this intention should show in the performance. My utterances must serve you and express my concern; they demand an attitude that phenomenally confirms the absoluteness of your existence. Not only must my speech respect your rights; as a philosopher, I offer you the universe of all that is philosophically relevant for human existence. In other words, your and my universe is the one that—in the dimension of the search for wisdom—is relevant for your and my lives. And I offer this to you from my point of view, recognizing that, though striving for impartiality, I cannot completely overcome my own biases, just as you probably cannot overcome yours.

All that has been formulated here with regard to "me," is equally valid for "you." While discussing philosophical issues with me, you, my interlocutor, are as conscious of my respectability as I am about yours. The mutuality of our respect and concern and our service to one another does neither level nor equalize us. You and I are connected by a double, chiastic asymmetry: your Youness—your absolute and a priori unicity, not your whims or wishes—demands me to serve you, just as I demand the same from you. The "highness" that constitutes You and Me commands me and you with equal force to look up to one another without destroying our equality in being at the same time lord and servant.[14] Not only am I as well a servant as a lord for You; I am both also for myself. For why should i be concerned about my own destiny, if it were not as absolute, high, and worthwhile as yours? My own absolute unicity makes me the servant of a dignity of mine in me that surpasses my own wishes and whims. My concern for my own meaningful existence cannot be understood if "I" myself am not simultaneously "high" and "low," commanding and obeying (or disobeying), obligating and performing, speaking and listening within myself.

What, how, who is the lordly highness, the demanding and commanding voice, the speaking dignity in you and me, to which i and you must listen? By turning me not only to You (and you to Me) but also me to Me and you to You, it lifts You and Me (or your and my "dignity") up *above* the economy of our (your and my and all others') patterns of sociality and communication. Or rather, it does not put us on a level *above* the social universe of which we are similar components: your and my and his and her "highnesses" decisively orient—and thereby grant meaning to—the society that we constitute by association and communication. Without that high and absolute dignity, there would still be a social life (higher than that of other animals), but we could not be concerned about any destiny; for destinies are unique and absolute, not properties or accidents of any social function, but worthwhile for themselves—as Kant would say: "ends in or by themselves."

Dear Reader

You are reading these lines here and now while I wrote them at another time, well before you read them. I, who here and now am writing, could also write: You will read these lines, which I write here and now, at a later time in another place, although it is not altogether excluded that then you will be seated in the chair and the room where I am writing now. Even then, however, your there and my here cannot coincide completely. Even if we are speaking to one another in a shared now, our bodies do not coincide and there is a temporal, albeit slight, difference between the thought that I express while you are listening, and your understanding. We alternate in speaking and listening, responding and re-responding, and that takes time. Thanks to our differences in space and time we are able to dialogue. However, your proximity would make it easier for me to be concerned about your singular existence than the idea that there might be at least one reader of these lines out there. Perhaps "you" do not exist: it is quite possible that nobody besides me will ever read what I am writing here and now. If I saw you exist and sit in front of me, not as an anonymous abstraction, but in real flesh, I would have at least a few clues about your destiny, which then I could address with concern and particular interest. True, even writing for an anonymous audience presupposes at least some picture of capable and preferred readers, but such a picture is only tentative and vague; it can easily turn out to be unrealistic.

How difficult is it to reproduce in writing the situation of a conversation from face to face! And how seductive is the isolation that writing demands! Don't we feel the pull to enclose ourselves within the boundaries of our private interests, word-and-thought patterns, obsessions, hobbies, repetitions, images, interests, and so on? Is narcissism already lurking in our simultaneously writing and reading what we write, even when—or exactly because—we accompany our writing with a critical eye and ear and a correcting pen?

The best chance of not betraying the conversational turn while writing seems to lie in letter writing, as we already mentioned. But even then you and I need a lot of conditions that warrant the genuineness of our exchange. For example, a common interest more particular and individual than the universal interest that brings all human individuals together, a common language (which does not exclude that you and i write in different languages), and a certain level of acquaintance with one another's situation and life story. But in any case—and this is as true of writing as it is of speaking to you—my narcissism is challenged by you and thus opened to you: not to your narcissist wishes or actions, but to that which is the best in you: your unique and absolute respectability. Your needs and wishes enable you to choose, but neither You nor I can be invented or inaugurated by you or me. You and I precede our preferences and exchanges; we are not free to accept or reject their factuality. All we can do is to agree or disagree with their apriority and then to realize it in the world. Disagreement does not abolish the undeniable force of this imposition, but rejoicing establishes us in peace.

When in philosophy I offer you my interpretation of all that seems interesting for you and me as representing humanity for and with one another, we submit the universe to the alliance through which You and I have brought me and you into conversation. The universe that mediates between your and my interpretations-in-conversation is limited in many ways: (1) the relevance it may have for humanity in all its cultural and historical varieties is filtered by your and my imagination; (2) we are children of our cultural and personal history; and (3) when we speak, our interests are codetermined (adjusted, widened as well as narrowed) by the interlocutor's interests. What you and I thus offer and propose is a doubly personalized world, the structures and features of which we may want to discuss, but our examination is performed in the form of continual invitations to responding, which invokes new responses—without end. No system or world picture can stand on its own; it can only be a proposal. That is, (1) it presupposes at least one respondent (who should be as philosophical as is necessary for understanding at least part of the proposed interpretation); (2) by inviting a discussion, it underlines the personal limitation of its content; (3) it affirms, in hope, that it may contribute to a serious approach of (the) truth; and (4) the act of proposing itself transcends the proposed ensemble (the "world" or "universe") by offering it as token of a desired engagement that offers us the opportunity to overcome our narcissistic desire to be, as solitary thinkers, on top of "it all."

If every philosophy is a proposal in wait for discussion, we must give up the classical portrait of the philosopher as a kind of hermit who from the top of his mountain maps the universe by ordering and analyzing all things (*ta panta*) as components of one whole (*to pan*). Every system should be prefaced by words that emphasize the "proposing" (or "propositional") and inviting character of the offered attempt. Dogmatism is an aberration because it identifies the subject of philosophy with one particular ego. Ongoing discussions are not possible, unless we are convinced that we *need* others in order to better discover the narrowings and mistakes that each thinker inevitably makes, especially in periods of solitude.

The virtues of periodic solitude should certainly not be bashed—silence and distance are necessary for diving under the commonplaces and slogans of the day—but the silence of wisdom is different from silent ignorance; it loves to talk philosophically to others who have lived through enough silence to generate the same kind of love.

If we continue to reserve the name "philosophy" for a parade of singular thinkers whose oeuvres form one museum or library or history of philosophy, the intersubjective and social life of thinking as conversation falls outside of philosophy. What name, then, should we use for that conversation? Is it the *real* history of philosophy? Must we maintain that the conversation constitutes philosophy as an ongoing confrontation of thinkers who are aware of their making history by speaking or writing to one another without end?

System and Dialogue

My experience of You is very different from the experience I have of myself. You are there, outside and in front of me; I am here, experienced by me from the inside. I see your face, whereas I never can see my face. I neither see myself in its entirety nor can see how I look when I look at someone else, whereas I see very well how you look at me or another person. When You address me, you impress me as worthy, surpassing all phenomena that belong to my world. Your presence commands me regardless of your function or position: whatever criminal or slave reveals my basic obligations as much as the emperor.[15]

Like any other conversation, a philosophical dialogue is structured and ruled by the chiastic asymmetry of You and me and Me and you: I respond to You, whose address urges me to provide a response that urges you to respond to Me. Our exchange exposes each of us to a demanding challenge: you and i must make ourselves vulnerable, while bringing to light how each one interprets human existence. All the levels from hostility and competition to friendship and love can be realized in this confrontation, but even in its most trusting forms the exchange remains a difficult adventure if it is pursued with appropriate passion.

Since You and I are philosophers, the temptation is great for each of us to escape from our confrontation by stepping up to a standpoint that may seem to represent a higher level of reflection—a point from which one can observe and explain what is going on between you and me in the dialogue in which we are engaged. This is the standpoint that, in fact, is described in the pages I am writing at this very moment. But have I then not failed again? I indeed have already escaped from the dialogue if my description is meant to be the final result of my questioning. However, it cannot be the final truth if I hope that someone else will read this writing. For such hope implies that I only am offering a proposal or—as in chess—trying out a move. Even conclusions are provisional: invitations in the hope that they will elicit a response from some known or as yet unknown You. Dialogues cannot be absorbed by any monologue because even a very long monologue—such as a book in ten volumes—cannot prevent becoming itself the first round of a new discussion. Only a monologue that does not become public at all—an unexpressed, silent monologue of the "soul with itself" can remain completely egoic and absolutely interior. But is such silence possible? Would it not express its findings indirectly or through other signs than words?

The idea of a complete and closed system tries to terminate all dialogues. It replaces the ongoing history of questioning and answering with a world in which there is no place for others than systematic leaders with their assistants and pupils. If such a system could be true, the history of thought would end with the scholastic celebration of its author's thought.

To the extent in which several systems are still competing with one another, they continue the dialogical tradition, but this is then understood as merely preparatory on the way to the ultimate truth, which—as we saw in chapter 1—can and should be thought and re-thought by all solitary egos. The truth would then declare all non-didactical dialogues superfluous. The search for truth would condemn us to repetition and application.

If we give up the idea of a final system because we think that the difference between you and me is fundamental not just for living, but also for philosophy, then dialogue is not only inevitable but also final. Every new thinker necessarily changes the conditions of philosophy and in every exchange I have to learn from you (just as you have to learn from me).

The philosophical conversation must try to integrate its best elements into higher syntheses, but the idea that it must culminate in *the* ultimate system of all human truth would lead to one of the following methods. (1) You and I could see our discussion as an exercise in the construction of a shared theory. This conception of the dialogue belongs to the definition of philosophy as a universally human system. (2) I *use* the conversation to enrich my philosophy, which, in the end, remains the property of an autonomous and solitary ego. In this case, the dialogue falls back on the model of a private egology. (3) You and I practice philosophy in the only form in which it happens, namely as a multiplicity of dialogues, but we have lost our orientation, because, more than ever, the ideal of a universally valid and convincing system seems unattainable.

To give up the ideal of a final system does not terminate the history of philosophy if the search for (more) truth is understood as a thoughtful movement that lies deeper than propositional and argumentative networks. If philosophy, more similar to human life itself than to the reflective methods and logics of thetic language, is a particular stylization of the conversation to which a shared desire for insight drives all human communities and associations, its meaning can be discovered through a—no less existential than cerebral—involvement in the ongoing discussions of our situation. Logic and method and all the refinements of their theses, strategies, and distinctions are indispensable for a philosophically updated practice of thinking, but they are not enough.

Conversation and Universality

However much I try to reach you, the singular reader you are, by writing this or any other essay or treatise, I fail. By publishing what I write, I necessarily address all possible readers, making them thus instances of a genus "the reader." I do know that each one's reading will be different, and to some extent I keep this in mind when using expressions that can easily be misunderstood, but I do not conduct a conversation with you, reader, this unique person here and now, who seem to be interested in this text. Speaking to you is different, not only because you can immediately answer, which then might trigger a dialogical to and fro, but primarily because my unique singularity addresses your singular unicity. A letter to you is the closest example of writing that conserves something of that double singularity, when the letter is clearly addressed and protected against reading by others. Letters can be published, however. An open letter is, of course, directed to all possible readers besides the person or the persons I want to target; but even love letters that are published lose their singularizing intimacy. If I published them, they already proclaim that I either wrote them as samples of a literary genre for public consumption or that they were sincere until the moment I decided to use them as texts for all readers who might savor them, including all those with whom I have no other relationship than their interest in reading and my interest in being read. If others publish someone's love letter, for example those of Hölderlin or Flaubert, their publication subordinates the erotic relationship of the writer to psychological, literary, aesthetic, historical, or philosophical interests. The singularity of the lovers then no longer exceeds their exemplification of "love" or "style" or "writing" or "intimacy" or "personal development" or some other essence.

Something similar happens if I write a book, for example an autobiography, as a uniquely personal gift or souvenir for one singular person, perhaps to be opened after my death. As soon as such a text were published, it would receive another, possibly universal meaning. This does not necessarily abolish the intimate meaning it has for the one to whom the writer addressed it, but it emphasizes the meanings that, within this former message to the only one, may interest others. The opposition between singularity and universality of meaning is not absolute. For all universality remains abstract and undecided unless it is consumed and transformed into a subordinate element of the uniquely singular existence of an irreplaceable person who appropriates it in a unique time and place. All texts must be singularized, whereas many intimate letters have a universal aspect; but, on the other hand, no singular insight can be isolated from its gestation during a period of communication with others who were searching in the same direction.

With regard to philosophy-as-conversation, the indications presented above seem useful for answering the question of what, exactly, we can learn from it. If all sharing of universally valid knowledge must result in insights of uniquely singular persons whose existential truth differs from the universal possibilities they discuss with one another, what more than a shared *preparation* for truth can we then expect from their conversation?

The advantage of conversation over solitary thought (which, in fact, is not even possible without continual reacting to other thinkers) can be sought in the fact that we always can learn from others, or in a consideration of all the dianoetic and ethical virtues (such as receptivity and humility) that are stimulated by interaction; but does the conversation also induce a conclusive knowledge or vision in each of the participants? Don't we observe that many philosophers with strong convictions avoid discussion? They may be formidable debaters but bad listeners. Does too much dialogue not lead to skepticism, while silence and concentration foster systematic coherence and a firm position?

Certainly, the importance of philosophical conversations does not lie in some democratic ideal, according to which everyone's speaking would be as true or promising as that of everyone else (which is obviously false). It is also false that discussion necessarily creates peace, which is one of the conditions for coming closer to truth. Though discussion indeed is much better than the isolation caused by an all-out war, speaking itself can be as destructive as the most powerful weapons. Rhetoric easily degenerates into silencing those who love truth alone.

Many conditions and virtues are indeed presupposed for a philosophical conversation on the way to (more) truth. All of them follow from the demands of truth itself. But if truth does not emerge unless it is at the same time *universal* (sharable by all who see it) and *unique* (singularized in the unique existence of this and that philosopher who transforms the sharable in a singular mode of a temporally and culturally particular figure of truth), then truth happens only "in" and "among" those who are virtuous and skilled enough to participate in a philosophical conversation about many approaches to the truth.

That all great philosophies are singular, unique, and of only one time is confirmed by the fact that they cannot be repeated by anyone but their authors. Platonists, Aristotelians, Thomists, Scotists, Spinozists, Kantians, Hegelians, Heideggerians, and other followers of their philosophical heroes are either epigones or commentators. As such, they deserve our gratitude for their useful transformation of the master's oeuvre into a (neo-Platonic, neo-Thomist, neo-Kantian, neo-Hegelian . . .) tradition. There is nothing wrong with representing a tradition, but even so, one produces new versions of the origin. The singularity of each version will be more or less remarkable as the representative's thought is more or less strong, deep, authentic, and original. Great re-thinkers such as Plotinus or Thomas (re)create new beginnings, but most of us must be content with a more pedestrian mode of participation in the history of philosophy. What we cannot do, and therefore should not want to do, is to restrict ourselves to merely historical reconstructions of past philosophies from a completely neutral and non-involved perspective. Such reconstructions are impossible, because a no man's perspective cannot be found. Each paraphrase or commentary is a re-creation with a past and future and a spirit of its own. Consequently, the difference in originality between commentators, epigones, and original thinkers is more gradual than radical. But certainly the distinction between powerful thinkers who present their own thoughts and all those individuals who study their works is clear. Whether the latter passionately defend their hero or combine their philosophical interest with critical distance, they try to find their own way of relating to the dissonant multiplicity of the contemporary currents that challenge their meditation. Whatever doubts may assail them, as long as they remain involved, their participation expresses a stance, an orientation, and a movement of their own, and this is their philosophical position, even if it cannot be formulated in the form of a doctrine or a vision.

Philosophy and Wisdom

Serious participation in the ongoing conversation that constitutes the real history of philosophy is experienced as an experiment in learning something deeper and more important than the transparency of a rigorously augmented doctrine. The ancients called it *sophia, sapientia*. *Philosophia* was an attempt to reach wisdom through, via, following but also surpassing the "epistemic" or "scientific" way of well-defined, well-observed, well-imagined, well-argued thought. Even Descartes, Spinoza, Kant, and Hegel (who in 1801 obtained his doctorate in *Weltweisheit* or "world wisdom") tried to become wise through participation in the practice of philosophy, just as their ancient and medieval predecessors. It was typical of modern philosophy, however, that the distance separating wisdom from the rigorously conducted and completed science of philosophy was thought to be minimal or non-existent. If modern philosophers had emphasized the role of affectivity and if their epistemology had paid more attention to the ethical and intuitive virtues that condition the way to wisdom, they might have shown that the method of philosophy cannot be reduced to conceptual and observational principia of thought. A logic of the "heart" in the line of Saint Augustine and Pascal would have shown, for example, how our "tasting" (*sapere*), challenged by the taste (*sapor*) of wisdom (*sapientia*), is essential for a real, fully integrated, concrete, and life-permeating knowledge, which otherwise remains abstract, cold, gamelike, and indifferent to the ways and meanings of human existence.

Not only tasting, but also touching, smelling—or, more generally, sensing—are necessary. Not only as a consequence or sequel of empirically and logically correct conclusions, but in the first place as access to the sources and as the basis of rigorous thinking. Good thought must not only "sink in" to become alive (operative, concrete, cordial, wise, and so on); but it also owes it departure—and all its redepartures after dead ends and readjustments—to "a kind of *aisthesis*"[16]—a good nose or taste, a sense that determines the direction and the quality of our basic assumptions.

The laboratories of "pure reason" have been secured as bunkers against the intrusions of the heart, because their officials were afraid that "subjective feelings" would disable their basic certainties.

Even now, after all the post-Hegelian critiques of their unproven assumptions, "arbitrariness" and "subjectivism" are the nicknames used to fence off serious consideration of the affective sources that feed all theory.

The difference between *scientia* (philosophy as "science") and *sapientia* (wisdom) is an experiential distinction. It is experienced, felt, undergone, tasted, but it cannot be captured in the categories and methodical devices of modern logic and scientific observation. Wisdom cannot be made or produced in the way we produce definitions, arguments, plans, or methods. A passionate dedication to the most rigorous forms of philosophical practice can make us wiser, even if it has not yet resulted in a final theory of one's own. Wisdom does not coincide with the absolute *Wissenschaft* of a coherent product, because it is not made, but *grows*. As all growth, its presence escapes our will and work. We may become aware of having become wiser than we were when we began to philosophize, but such awareness has always an amazing aspect and it is difficult to explain what, exactly, we have learned.

Wisdom in philosophy can be compared with the excellence gained (acquired-and-received) by great pianists, composers, painters, cooks, carpenters, tennis players, dancers, and so on. Even if the recipe for sublimity is 98 percent sweat plus 2 percent inspiration, the latter is not only indispensable but decisive. The hard work demanded for acquiring the appropriate skills must be accompanied by an element—something like a force, sense, spirit, excellence, *arete*, *virtus*, or virtuality—that has its own advancement and intensification, while we, the self-conscious thinkers, are moved by our striving and struggling for skillful perfection. When awareness of having grown in wisdom surprises us, we cannot say when exactly we made progress and what addition to our former knowledge constituted this progress. We are now more experienced in thinking than before: we are more confident because we know how to handle (at least some) problems; we feel up to the tasks and our standards for excellence have become different from, but not more lax than, those that were formulated in the handbooks of logic and methodology. We want philosophy to be more interesting and better than correct: not only rigorous, but also existentially relevant, inspiring, beautiful, splendidly true.

Whereas we concentrate on the questions and proposed answers that make up the field of our discipline, the decisive part of our growth in truth has its own time and change underneath the level of our explicit self-awareness. At some moments we feel "warm," closer to the truth, or rather "cold" and lost, without real rapport to the "thing itself" that we want to pursue. Does our approach of the truth happen in the dark, just as dreams? But how then can we be confident that we are growing or have grown in wisdom? Are the rationalists not right in warning us against the arbitrariness of our imagination?

By interpreting our dreams and illusions as masks and distorted messages from the unconscious, Freud and others have tried to liberate their truth by translating it in understandable constellations that make sense. The sense they sought was visible from the perspective they, the analysts, found meaningful. They thought that their method could be developed into a fundamental theory of human nature.

Is a metaphilosophical analysis possible of the growth to wisdom, which occurs in the night that accompanies our philosophical self-awareness? Can we transpose the half-hidden process of maturing thought to the transparent dimension of self-conscious philosophy? For example, could and should philosophy refound itself by translating the laws of growth toward truth into the philosophical language(s) with which we are acquainted? If so, would we then have found the gate to the absolutely fundamental and final *episteme*? Would such a metaphilosophy itself not again be originated and driven by a deeper and unconscious truth?

Truth and Conversation

If the truth cannot be captured in the language of traditional philosophy, because it approaches us in a deeper, obscure but cordial dimension, and if the philosophical conversation is motivated by the hope that it can bring us closer to the truth, then it is possible to answer the question of why philosophical conversations are better than monologues.

We have said that the search for the truth demands many singular approximations, which cannot be synthesized into one final, all-embracing system or doctrine. Someone who is convinced that philosophy (in the traditional, modern sense of this practice) is the highest possibility of human truth, could attack this statement by concluding that it proposes a self-contradictory form of relativism because it defines truth as a multiple disagreement about the one and all-encompassing truth. The attacker could try to find a common denominator in all the proposed philosophies in order to show that at least some truths are universally recognized. If those who are disappointed by the poverty of such a shared conviction dismiss his appeal to a generally accepted core of truth, the challenger might insist on the task of overcoming the differences by further investigations, which might lead to skepsis or victory.

Another response to relativism is attempted by those who continue to defend the truth monopoly of one coherent system while condemning all other positions as errors or deviations insofar as they disagree with the only fully true philosophy.

If truth does not let itself be captured by the experiential and logical structure of philosophy, but rather affects us on a deeper level, from which it then sends flashes and glimpses to the surface of self-aware perception, conceptuality, and language, then philosophical relativism itself is a meaningful phenomenon, insofar as its real and fundamental contradictions refer us to that obscure but less superficial underground in which all philosophical self-awareness is rooted, even if it is unaware of its roots. The roots through which the trees of philosophy are fed are intertwined with a fertile soil that has a history of its own: the hidden history of truth underneath the level of our discussions. In order not to succumb to skepticism, the hope that motivates our conversation points to some kind of presence through which the truth attracts all singular thinkers via their own, unique, and necessarily different affective and imaginative as well as cognitive approaches, thus gathering them without allowing them to reduce the truth itself to one of their theories. Somehow all wisdom-loving searches must converge despite their explicit and implicit divergences. Without some kind of trust in the possibility of getting closer to truth when all conditions of good thought are fulfilled, philosophical life becomes incomprehensible and impossible. Skeptical despair is refuted by the experience of thinking, insofar as the latter reaches further and deeper than correctly thinking itself.

Another metaphilosophical postulate of the hope that drives the philosophers and their discussions follows from this basic trust. If proximity to truth cannot be defined by any theory, conceptuality cannot be the very dimension in which the truth happens. Conceptual language may be indispensable to manifest the comprehensible aspect of the truth, but the very multiplicity and untranslatability of its other aspects and modes of manifestation testify against the possibility of identifying the truth as a conceptual reality. Besides philosophy, there are many other modes of making the truth apparent to our thought and senses: architecture, poetry, theater, painting, meditation, walking, hospitality, and so on. All of them are modes of showing what we—even without concepts or words—can understand as more or less true and surprisingly meaningful. How many possible and real works in each of these dimensions testify to the truth of the last sentences! Neither *dianoia* nor *logos* present us with the one and ultimate truth itself. If the truth is one, it cannot be said or thought.

Nevertheless we can refer to it, and philosophy, the discipline of thinking according to the most refined logic, is one of the most sublime and delightful possibilities of referential evocation, but must we, in the end, not be content with a multiplication of representations that refer to the truth by breaking its light in a variety of approximate manifestations?

Participation

The truth does not manifest itself in the form of a system. Its attraction keeps us on the way and together by stimulating us to approach it in the every time unique but solidary modes that are given to us. Our differences do not impede convergence; if our search is well-oriented, we may hope that serious approaches do neither destroy nor diminish, but instead display the abundance of a truth that surpasses conceptual synthesis. Perhaps we may even state that all approaches to the truth—including its distortions—refer us to it, if we are able to read them as attempts that express at least some desire of some truth. Similar to vices that use the mask of virtue, or to kitsch that imitates great art, false opinions try to seduce us by appearing to be true. If they are accompanied by arguments or descriptions, they might contain useful hints.

After having affirmed and confirmed many times with great conviction the necessity of rigorous logical and methodical conditions of good work in philosophy, one must be allowed to state with equal force that approximation of the truth demands more, not less, than professional skills and passion: participation in a dialogical history that leads beyond all theory toward an experiential acquaintance with thinking together toward a wiser mode of dealing with truth and destiny. What occurs in the depth "underneath" and "above" the logical level of our discussions is "greater" and "better" than all that can be known philosophically, but since it is more desirable—lovable beyond all philosophy—we can grow in familiarity with it through the learned ignorance of a thought that, through conversation, develops into shared contemplation.

Contemplation or Colloquium?

The present chapter has pleaded for a dialogical practice and conception of philosophy. If the word "contemplation" was sometimes used, the purpose was to underline yet another aspect of thinking: its links to the universal and individual quest for personal wisdom. Actually, the word "contemplation" is commonly used as a synonym for survey or meditation, both of which can be performed by solitary thinkers. The contemplative tradition of Western civilization, however, cannot be understood as a succession of egocentric ruminations or egological treatises. From Parmenides and Plato on, its representatives addressed their words to others after having listened to their masters and interlocutors. Among these they invoked not only various fellow humans, but also some gods or even God. Exemplary texts, such as Augustine's *Confessions* and Anselm's *Monologion* (!), show that the inner dialogues of their authors served to share with others—disciples, parishioners, colleagues, and so on—what their own meditations had clarified. Moreover, their meditating was not merely a solitary confrontation with the depths of their soul; it was framed and punctuated by invocations of God, whose words they pondered while mobilizing their affective and intellectual skills to hear and answer the appeal that touched them. Their thinking was interwoven with prayer: a "listening" and "responding" that attuned their "soul" to a divine interpellation.

Is it possible to hear God speak—to listen and to respond well or badly? Is a dialogical thinking possible not only with myself, or with you, but also with God? Is such a dialogue desirable, perhaps even necessary, to find my place and yours in the universe and in philosophy?

The following chapter is dedicated to an exploration of the conditions which would allow for statements like the following: God speaks; we can hear God's Word. Thinking about God presupposes listening and responding to God's speaking presence. Speaking about

God fails if it is not redeemed by adoration. *Philosophia* cannot ignore—it cannot even be performed well without—prayer.

Since such statements are uncommon and shocking, especially in philosophy, my attempt at answering some of the questions involved must proceed cautiously and begin with some basic observations that, I hope, are not too controversial. Let us then begin with philosophy's attitude regarding God and theology.

FOUR

From Thinking to Prayer

Philosophy and Theology

From 600 B.C. to the nineteenth century, few European philosophers have denied the existence and the workings of God, gods, or other divine powers. How could they be sure that they were not appealing to illusions or empty names? Did their beliefs rest on proofs? Although some of them tried to construe such proofs, even most of them already presupposed the existence of their divinities when they entered the realm of philosophy. That they also wanted to demonstrate that their belief was rational cannot surprise us, but we have become more skeptical with regard to the validity of their proofs. Are we more critical or less intelligent? Were they biased, or were they gifted with a speculative insight that we have lost?

Study of all philosophical theologies is necessary for a thorough critique of the arguments they use to ascertain the belief that they seem to have imported from elsewhere—from a religious tradition or "faith"—into philosophy. Some philosophers, such as Leibniz and Hegel, while recognizing that they, like everyone, began with a naïve belief in God, claimed that they were able to transform their initial naïveté into the conclusion of a rigorous demonstration. Others maintain a margin of incomprehensibility with regard to the essential determinations of the God in whom they believe, while remaining convinced that his/her/its existence can be proved. Again others have given up the hope that any proof can be given, although they continue to appeal to their religious faith for the orientation of their personal life and—at least marginally—as ultimate horizon of their philosophy.

This chapter is neither dedicated to a discussion of various "proofs" for the existence of God, nor to the question of whether it is possible at all to discover God by way of finite syllogisms. The question I would like to answer instead asks how philosophical thought should deal with God, if God exists. Aware of the many meanings of the words "God" and "existing," we must, however, clarify how we want to understand them in this chapter, and this demands a narrowing of our subject.

It is obvious that the generic meanings of "the divine," "the God," "the gods," just as the generic meaning of "religion," hardly suffice for any accuracy about "the" arguments or proofs that are used to clarify or justify certain beliefs. Even the word "God," as used in modern philosophy alone, covers several, radically different, meanings. A "phenomenology" of God—more or less inspired by Hegel's *Phenomenology of the Spirit*, could unfold a whole array of meanings, beliefs, and theologies that we should traverse before writing a treatise about God in any determinate sense of the word. Such a "history of God" would certainly be illuminating, but I will not try to develop it here, because the detour would be too long for this book.

The only God that interests us here and now is the God who, according to the Christian faith, is revealed in Jesus, the Christ, as celebrated in his Church. God's originary and all-permeating relevance implies that God's existence determines the heart and the entire life of all persons whose faith refers them to this God. In order to study the relations between faith in God and philosophy, I will focus on their tight union in the person of a philosopher who happens to be a Christian (or rather, a Christian who happens to be a philosopher). The perspective from which I approach this "topic"—and this is a further delimitation—is the perspective of this book: what role does *speaking* play and how does it unfold in dealing with the *God* of Jesus Christ?

In order to prevent confusions that plague many debates on the relations between God, religion, faith, philosophy, and theology, let us begin with a few distinctions among the latter three modes of acquaintance: faith, philosophy, and theology.

Christian faith (which, in the following pages, I shall name "faith" without qualification) is not a theory or system and not in the first place a body of knowledge. It is the confident acceptance through which a human heart answers God's self-presentation in Jesus Christ, the Word through which God created the world and the mediator through whose death and resurrection the Spirit unites human lives with God's. Faith is trust and allegiance, belonging to God in confidence and fidelity. But it has its own gnosis.[1]

As *credere in* God (and not as a mere belief that certain propositions are true while others are anathema), faith does not need scientific, philosophical, or theological skills to "know" what it trusts or to faithfully practice the imperatives that are implied in this trust. When Christian faith spread in the Hellenistic world, it borrowed philosophical elements from Greek and Jewish philosophers to express and clarify the gnosis that was implied in its own stories, poems, prayers, and practices. With the help of these *spolia gentium*[2] it developed arguments of its own in various versions of *philosophia* which we, postmoderns, would rather call theological, because the "philosophical" arguments they (e.g., Origen, the Cappadocians, Augustine) used were intertwined with data from revelation.

Philosophy in the modern sense of the word is a legacy of "the Greeks." Although recently much too much emphasis has been put on its "typically Greek" character (even by authors whose acquaintance with Greece, Rome, and the Biblical tradition is not ascertained) and not enough on the transformative powers that have changed Greek philosophy during the more than one thousand years between Parmenides and Proclus, it is true that the European figure of Christianity is unthinkable without that heritage.

Under the influence of the *modern* idea of philosophy, many historians of philosophy have stated that the difference between Greek and Christian *philosophia* lies in the fact that the latter is philosophical in name only, because it is based on faith, whereas the Greek one is autonomous, just as is modern philosophy. This is a mistake: the philosophy from Parmenides and Heracleitus to Proclus is steeped in myths and beliefs and, more fundamentally, in a religious faith or trust that implies its own cosmic and supracosmic divinities. As I will argue further on, no faithless philosophy is possible, and this is confirmed by thorough study of any single great philosophy.[3]

Theology is the reflective discipline that tries to understand and explain what God has revealed throughout history about the truth that is needed for a true and good human life. Insofar as faithful persons also reflect on the relevance of that truth for their own and others' lives in the world, each believer is a more or less advanced theologian, but one does not have to be a professional thinker to lead a faithful existence. Whether the community of Christians needs professional theologians who are skilled in the noetic disciplines of their cultural surroundings is another question, but even if this is the case, it will be difficult to prove that such theologians must be formed in the "typically Greek" style of thought. The historical developments of Europe have conditioned a Christian theology that is marked by the integration of Greco-Roman thought, because this style of thought was dominant in the world where the Christian message was embraced; but if other styles of thought are equally possible, faith is universal and divine enough to convert them into elements of its own elaborations. Although faith cannot express itself without borrowing from particular cultures, it cannot idolize any of them. Its catholicity opens faith to all nations and times, whereas philosophy and theology, like languages, are necessarily particular and mortal. Consequently, the essential distance of faith with regard to all theologies and philosophies must be emphasized as much as its historical borrowings from established cultures. Its incultured "eternity" separates faith itself from all philosophical or theological doctrines or systems, even if the expression *"philosophia perennis"* is meaningful insofar as it points at a certain continuity of thought, despite the great variety of theories in which it has unfolded.

After the Hellenistic period, and especially during the so-called Middle Ages, Christianity concentrated on the critical appropriation of its Greco-Roman heritage. Instead of remaining a proudly independent search for the highest form of wisdom, philosophy was submitted to a higher discipline: the theological explanation of the revealed wisdom as received and lived in the community of the faithful under the guidance of the very spirit who had inspired that revelation. Periodically philosophy reasserted its independence, but on the whole its subordination to theology was reinforced, while both disciplines recognized that faith itself, as a God-given grace, did not have to compete with the groping of theoretical reflection.

A new phase in the history of faith and thought began when philosophers reclaimed their independence from both theology and faith, in order to discover what autonomous thought had to say about truth and wisdom. Most philosophers of the modern era did not reject their allegiance to Christianity, but autonomous concentration on their own program—and encouragements from the side of a modern kind of theology that insisted on a clear distinction between "supernatural" faith and "natural" reason—favored the development of a fully emancipated and in the long run Godless philosophy.

The new situation that issued from the growing estrangement between theology and philosophy was uncomfortable for Christians who practiced philosophy. Those who did not want to accept a separation could still pursue the ideal of an encompassing form of contemplation, within whose theological horizon they would develop strictly philosophical theses that fitted the overall purpose. But which philosophical community satisfied the conditions of their ideal? Plato and Aristotle had already been baptized by the great medieval thinkers. It is therefore not surprising that most philosophers who remained loyal to the tradition of one encompassing theology continued the heritage of Thomas or Scotus or some other medieval school. More adventurous philosophers, who also did not give up their loyalty to Christian faith, had to cope with a cultural shift that seemed to exclude the reproduction of premodern thought. If they themselves were not giants of thinking, to which philosophical tradition could they turn to receive inspiration and support?

In fact we see that, after Nicholas of Cusa (1401–1464), neither theology nor philosophy generated great thinkers among Catholics. Theology lost its intimacy with the mystical tradition, while reproducing old questions and doctrines with superficial adaptations to the epistemological demands of the moderns. In the meantime, the mainstream of modern philosophy, greatly impressed by the rebirth of the sciences, took a decidedly anthropocentric turn by advancing from program to program and from system to system toward a world-centered responsibility without God.

Those Christian philosophers who did not set their hope on a reproduction of medieval traditions found themselves in a bind: if philosophy could develop itself in an autarchic way, what or who could then guarantee that it would not contradict orthodox theology and faith itself? That the fear of such contradictions was not imaginary would soon be confirmed by the course that modern philosophy took from the seventeenth to the twentieth century. However, the climate among Christians was still optimistic; philosophy, if well performed, could not contradict the revealed truth of God-given faith and would certainly fit a well-thought theology. Catholic theology of the seventeenth century justified this expectation by its theory about the relations between "nature" and "supernatural" grace. According to this theory, philosophical thinking, even for Christians, was confined to "purely natural" reason; its task was to discover those truths that (a) could be discovered by reason on its own, and that (b) were presupposed by the acceptance of faith in the "supernatural" revelation that God gave in addition to his (equally free) gift of creation. Among the insights that "natural reason" could prove, God's existence and the immortality of the human soul were considered to be the main truths that philosophy should demonstrate.

Few non-Catholic philosophers of the last four hundred years have proposed theories that were welcomed by the Catholic theologians of that same period. Only Catholic philosophers seemed "natural" enough to be able to serve their theology with convenient philosophies (which, in fact, usually smelled somewhat musty). Was the reason of most or all non-Catholic philosophers from Spinoza to Nietzsche too blinded to follow the "natural" course of reasoning? But how then were the Catholics preserved from such denaturation? Did their faith make their reason more natural than that of the others?

Today few Catholic philosophers are convinced that they can or must prove the existence of God and the immortality of the soul in order to accomplish their philosophical task or their duties with regard to the Church. The whole idea of such *"praeambula fidei,"* as the Thomists called it, has become outlandish. Even many good theologians strongly doubt or deny that the "God of the philosophers" must be presupposed in order to be capable of believing in the God of Jesus Christ.

Should Catholic philosophers be recalled to order and made again obedient to the demands of theology? Or should theologians first of all listen to the philosophers and ask what *they* have experienced about their own abilities and results?

Before we try to answer this question, we must be well aware of the historical situation and the theoretical framework within which we want to approach it. In a homogeneously Christian society, the relationship between philosophy and theology can be studied as the relation between two levels of reflection about and around a basic faith that is shared by all or most intellectuals. For a believer, it is rather obvious that theology represents a higher dimension of reflection, which integrates the best of philosophy in order to understand as much as possible the truth of faith. Within this general horizon, philosophers have a subordinate task (theologians may call it a charisma). Certainly, opinions can differ as to the questions of (1) whether the domain of philosophical questions extends farther than those of the questions that emerge from faith, and (2) how dependent and independent philosophers should be with regard to theology. The first question can be answered if we can be sure that there are interesting and meaningful questions without intrinsic links to faith. I will leave this question open. The second question is not so pressing within a homogeneously Christian society, although even there it sometimes becomes urgent, as it did, for example, during the medieval struggle between the *facultas artium* and the *facultas sacrae doctrinae*. Since the beginning of modernity, however, the question has become decisive. Theology and philosophy have parted ways; philosophy has shown its force in monumental works of great thinkers, while theology seems to have lost much of its inspiration. Philosophy has constituted itself as a Republic of universal thought with its own program, plans, convictions, institutions, rules, rights, traditions, and authorities, all of which express a certain mentality, a specific ethos, a characteristic spirit, and a profound kind of (non-Christian, but typically philosophical) trust or faith. Catholics, who in these circumstances participate in the history of philosophy, belong not only to their community of religious faith but also to the republic that is based on philosophical faith. Is the latter compatible with the former?

This question is no longer a question about two levels within one Christian culture. Instead, it focuses on a double participation in two communities with their own histories and traditions and exemplary heroes.[4] The differences between these communities are obvious, but their compatibility is not. In order to know what I am and how I should think as a person who is at the same time a Catholic and a philosopher, I must take a clear position with regard to both allegiances. Assuming that I do not want to be separated from the community of the faithful, we can simplify the question by asking what this loyalty implies with regard to my participation in the ongoing history of philosophy.

The Republic of Philosophy

As a member of the philosophical community, I share in its work: the thoughtful conversation described in the former chapters. There was a time that philosophers were seen as lonely thinkers in ivory towers, building systems out of almost-nothing according to the self-evident rules of their autonomous reason. We have seen that this kind of autonomy has never been realized, because all thinkers were—and probably will always be—codetermined by communal and historical peculiarities. The modern idea of philosophy may include the individualized autonomy of universally valid and controllable truth, but the reality to which that idea led was a particular, dominantly Western, community that slowly emancipated itself from its Christian past in order to take the shape of a modern republic with an ethos and a code of mores, tastes, rights, and duties of its own.

The idea of autonomy in thought and behavior has not died. It has changed into the idea of a shared kind of communal and historical autonomy: all who are able and willing to accept human thought as the supreme judge about truth and decency form a sovereign community that investigates and evaluates all nations, churches, cultures, and beliefs from the height of its universally valid tribunal. The right to thinking on our own is guaranteed by its faith in human self-determination.

If we let the most famous thinkers of the last centuries speak in the name of this republic, human freedom and self-realization forbid us to constantly look up to a superhuman sovereignty that would demand obedience. Most of those famous thinkers see the existence of an almighty, all-knowing, and creating God or god as an obstacle to human freedom. They seem to think that loyalty to humanity implies hostility or indifference toward religion, while obedience to a church that claims to know the most important truths about human destiny only awakens their pity or contempt.

Being Christian and Philosopher

If this rudimentary description of the contemporary situation of philosophy is more or less correct, how then can Christians be citizens of that philosophical community? Can they provisionally accept the ethos of "the philosophers" as long as they do not subscribe to theories or injunctions that clearly contradict their faith? Post-medieval theology seemed to open the possibility of some accommodation through its separation of "natural reason" from faith. However, it also demanded that philosophers should prove the existence of God. Can Christian philosophers, on this point, form a dissident group within the worldwide republic named Philosophy? Will they not be seen, treated, and avoided as a fifth column of spies or traitors? More importantly, are they sincere and profound philosophers if they consider their relation to God to be just "a point" that can be kept in the margins or reserved for later?

I have already suggested—and I will return to this—that the program of modern philosophy by itself tends to exclude and erase the question of God.[5] If this is true, the evolution of philosophy from seventeenth-century onto-theo-logy to twentieth-century Godlessness could be understood as a historically plausible (and in this sense "natural") unfolding of an areligious, or even antireligious, germ inherent to the emancipatory program of modernity.

It is easy to correct my description of the philosophical republic that emerged from modern philosophy by underlining that many of its citizens still believe in God (or in one of his imitations). However, the real question is whether such belief—which cannot be sincere if it does not permeate the believer's life—expresses itself in their philosophy. If it doesn't, their philosophy is either not radical, or it is an undigested lump in their self-consciousness.

Another objection against the offered description lies in a redescription of the last two hundred years as a genealogy of several philosophical communities, each of which has its own position vis-à-vis religion and faith. However, such a view does not yet explain the puzzling fact that the philosophies forwarded by Catholic thinkers of the last centuries strike us as poor and marginal in comparison with the leading thinkers, who no longer adhered to the Christian tradition. Why did the great tradition of Christian thought—in theology as well as in philosophy—lose its originality and inspiration after the emergence of modern science and philosophy?

Many reasons can be proposed to explain the major shift that puzzles us. Since I am not a historian, I will not try to sort them out,[6] but one aspect of the shift is clear: a new experience of human freedom as the source of inalienable rights.

Free Thinking as a Right

With regard to thinking, modern freedom signifies in the first place that we have the right to think on our own, individually and together. Whether philosophy, as autonomous thought, should include a (philosophical) theory about God is a question that has been debated since the beginning of Western thought, especially in the Christian theologies that emerged from it. This debate cannot be finished by quoting Feuerbach or Nietzsche or by a mixture of indifference and ignorance about the history of the question at stake.

One of the mistakes that threaten the discussion about the relation between God's and human freedom is to think of both as opposed within an encompassing horizon (the horizon of modern philosophy, as explained in chapter 2). Indeed, such opposition inevitably reduces God to a finite reality—however big, great, perfect, super, or all-surpassing this reality may be thought to be. By being distinguished from something other with which God would share one universe, God would be represented as a finite part of the totality, albeit the highest or supreme one, and much bigger or more important than the remaining portion of beings. That many thinkers have rejected God because they thought that there is not enough space for human freedom if God is infinitely sovereign, lawgiver, lord, and creator is a consequence of the widespread belief or fear that God's existence, as the summit (i.e., the supreme part) of the universe, would take away some significance or being from other parts. This belief, whether found among Christians or its enemies, lacks elevation and profundity because it is unable to question (and thus think beyond) the limits (i.e., the inherent finitude) of the universe, thus missing the infinitely more profound and uplifting orientation toward the Incomparable. The mistake that lies in that false belief may have many causes, for example a bad education in theology or inability to make sense of infinity in a non-mathematical sense; but the result is clear: a God who rivals with, diminishes, or represses human greatness, power, beauty, dignity, or freedom must be disliked in the name of Humanity. Faith in human dignity and freedom cannot but protest against faith in such a great but finite and tyrannical God! Even other faiths—such as faith in Nature, the Cosmos, Matter, Energy, Reason, History, Evolution, Progress, the Substance, the Spirit, or other quasi-Infinites—seem more acceptable than trust in a God who does not like the full unfolding of human liberty—unless, of course, the belief in God-as-competitor is utterly superficial and mistaken.

One does not have to deny that God exists as infinite and ultimate, uniquely and absolutely Absolute in order to affirm humanity's freedom and full responsibility in its own dimension. How exactly God's sovereignty and human freedom relate to one another is a question that cannot be adequately explained because the former is infinite and therefore incomparable to the finite universe of finite beings, about which it is easier to think. Even though we are able to meaningfully and correctly *refer to* the infinite, we are too finite to have a determinate concept of it. The medieval and modern controversies about the compatibility of human freedom with God's freedom have not led to clear conclusions, but neither have they been useless. At the least, they have shown that Christians, too, must honor human freedom and the ("natural") rights it implies. The right to free thought, as one of freedom's implications, has been claimed fiercely and joyfully by all who hated the Church for its authoritarian manners, later followed by many Christians who were not impressed by the scientific, philosophical, and, yes, theological wisdom of ecclesiastical bureaucracies. The right to think freely is cherished by all true philosophers as the essential source of their activity and professional honor. They must define it against all attempts at tutelage from the outside.

How do and how should Christian philosophers deal with the claim and honor of free thought? Although they are aware of our "postlapsarian" condition, they remain confident that the passion for truth will keep them well oriented. When theologians admonish them, they are not necessarily impressed, because contemporary theology, another human endeavor of finite understanding, has not shown any superiority in logical and experiential skills that would justify its guiding role within philosophy. However, the close contact with faith that theology is supposed to maintain (although this contact is not always apparent) lends some degree of authority to it with regard to the orthodoxy or heterodoxy of certain positions, but only faith itself is the absolute criterion for both theology and philosophy, as long as one adheres to it.

Faith versus Survey

How then does faith itself relate to the epistemic abilities of philosophy and theology? If faith is not a theory or belief system, as we stated above, how then can faith judge any -logy or -sophy? Should it not first produce its own experiential and logical translation before it can encounter philosophical and theological elaborations? But what if the concretization of faith into experience and logos has its own *pre*philosophical and *pre*theological mode of experiencing, practicing, and speaking? That faith is able to produce these is obvious if children and uneducated people can be initiated to it and become holy. It is even more obvious and attested by the most uncontested authority for anyone who reads the gospels.

In a more secular vein, we must focus on the radical difference between the intentionality of faith and that of any -logy, be it science, philosophy, or theology. As long as the modern model of study and research, as described in chapter 2, sets the stage, even for the understanding of faith, it inhibits an adequate relationship to God. The panoramic, observing, thematizing, and egological framework reduces faith to a belief or non-demonstrated opinion (*doxa*). If such a belief seems warranted by the authority of trustworthy persons, it is not unreasonable to adhere to it, but where, then, is God, who cannot be caught as a thing or theme or finite person? Within the indicated setting, the belief in a thematized God is treated as an unproved (and eventually improvable) thesis, which, in association with other proved or unproved but warranted theses, yields a coherent system that seems to represent the truth. Further on we will have to see what such a system of truth means for the meaning of God and all the theses that represent the relations of humanity, world, and history to God.

If, however, faith is *not* a belief (although it does imply and generate certain beliefs), but primarily the basic response of an entire person to God whose presence is experienced through signs, words, surprising events, etc. as an invitation to confidence and trust, then the entire framework of the universe changes. Rather, the framework of modern universality loses its all-encompassing character, because the ultimate horizon is no longer found in the limit of a universal space or universe, but instead in the lived face-to-face with the hidden but ultrapresent God, who always already has affected and welcomed and challenged me. No longer am I the stage director who dominates the universal scene, where both God and I play roles. Now I am just this i who stands before the hidden face of God, overwhelmed and delivered over to One to whom all horizons refer, without ever capturing or encircling this One, as if it ever could appear as a determinate figure within any universe.

What is a contradiction from the perspective of the philosophical staging reveals itself as a possibility of thought. As long as philosophers stand at the top of their panopticon, they inevitably think of the totality as encompassed by an ultimate horizon. There is nothing behind this horizon, but it remains tempting to look for a farther, still forgotten but transcendentally effective and perhaps discoverable horizon or dimension, which then would encompass a wider totality. However, since Plato, philosophers have pointed to something that is radically different, not only from all figures, appearances, or beings, but also from all horizons, a mysterious X—the Good, the One, the Unknown—*beyond* the totality of all that is and can be known. How can we think such a beyond, if the scope of thinking is limited to the universe? If the stage of philosophy excludes anything that surpasses the totality of all totalities, and if God is infinite, then there is no way to discover God from within the boundaries of any philosophical context or horizon.

However, what cannot be thought in the theater of panoramic objectification is possible, natural, and quite appropriate for the attitude or intentionality of faith. If God is encountered as the one who touches, awakens, provokes me, this event changes everything, beginning with the entire theater in which my universe unrolls its history. There is no longer any final horizon, because the universe displays the essential finitude of its composite totality, thus referring to the incomparable Other that cannot be part of it, although it is present in every one of its moments and details. Since Heidegger, some have tried to cope with the contradictory structure that shocks philosophy when it dares to ask ultimate questions, by calling the beyond "Nothing" or "the Nothing." That this Nothing is neither anything nor nothing is clear, if it is true that it "no-things" and that this "activity" grants being and a mixture of light and obscurity to all that is. Some interpreters have looked for traces of Christian faith in Heidegger's "nihilism," but it does not seem possible to liberate philosophy from the contradictions that beset it, as long as it persists in its attempt to capture not only the universe, but also its origin.

When God is no longer sought as an element or summit that belongs to the universe, but rather as the One to whom we can turn and refer because it turns to us, this turning is the ultimate and unsurpassable perspective that shows the finitude of all totalities by granting us an infinite openness without horizon. The Infinite refuses to become a component of any universe by locating all universes in a non- or "hyper"-universal (non-)space and (non-)time of infinity.

Early Christians who were aware of the Neoplatonic elucidations that contrast the relations of emanation and ascent with the noetic *kosmos* of beings, have borrowed from them for their theological explanations of their own Christian faith. It is not necessary to revive the discussion about the transformation that "Greek" philosophy thereby underwent if today we want to know how Christian faith feels about itself in relation to God who transcends all horizons.

Faith and Adoration

At the end of his third *Metaphysical Meditation*, presuming that he has proven the existence of God, Descartes takes "some time for the contemplation of this entirely perfect God, to ponder leisurely his wonderful attributes, to consider, admire, and adore the incomparable beauty of this immense light, at least as much as the force of my spirit, which remains blinded by it, will allow me. For, as faith teaches us that the supreme felicity of the other life consists in nothing else than this contemplation of the divine Majesty, so we experience now already that a similar, though incomparably less perfect, meditation allows us to enjoy the greatest delight of which we are capable in this life."[7]

Descartes does not seem troubled by any Pascalian contrast between "the God of the philosophers" and the God of Jewish and Christian faith. Was his philosophical reflection on the "idea of the infinite," found as naturally given in human conscience, enough to show the complete "perfection" and all "the wonderful attributes," "the incomparable beauty," and the "immense," blinding light of God? Or did the existence of "the infinite" refer him immediately to the God of his faith, whom—in accordance with the rules of his *Discourse on Method*—he had bracketed before beginning his proof of God's existence?[8] In any case, he seems to recognize that faith alone is enough to adore God and enjoy this adoration. He also affirms that the idea of the infinite belongs to the essence of human consciousness, but he does not thematize the difference between his philosophical search and the contemplative adoration, for which he takes a break in the middle of his metaphysical exercises.

This difference must be described and analyzed, if we want to know what philosophy (in its post-Cartesian mode) can and cannot know, and how it relates to the knowledge that is implied in adoration—or, in more generic terms, in prayer. A first approach is possible by recourse to the difference between speaking *about* and speaking *to*, as analyzed in the preceding chapters. If philosophy is not imprisoned in universal finitude, but reaches out to God, it culminates in thinking and speaking *about* God. Speaking *to* God, however, occurs in prayer, not in (modern) philosophy. Does God speak in prayer?

If we understand "speaking" as an illuminating metaphor for God's turning to the person who prays, the answer is: Yes; God has already spoken, awakened, and provoked the praying person before she, by way of answering, began to pray. Does God speak in philosophy? Modern philosophers are too focused on their themes and topics to notice a "Voice" or "Word" from the other side; if they talk about God, they make God their infinite Object. But that is enough to make him disappear, as we have seen a while ago. Only a non-thematizable God can escape the finitude of all totalities. Only an infinitely mysterious God to whom one is committed deserves the name "God."

Prayer is the clearest expression of Christian faith. To understand what it does and expresses, we must clarify the attitudinal constellation in which both unfold. Faith is the basic response to God's approach. Since God is invisible, his/her/its proximity cannot be noticed without signs, words, hints, or referring experiences, through which God's presence as an address or "call" is "revealed." Signs are not enough, however; they must also be recognized as such, and this presupposes a receptivity that is granted rather than conquered. When God's "speaking" is "heard," a response is inevitable, albeit in the form of a more eager ear, indifference, or avoidance. Normally a mixture of profound fear, awe, and amazing joy would follow from the confrontation with such majesty. Christian faith responds to the presentation of God's "Word" through participation in the communal, historical, and transhistorical union with the life of Jesus Christ. Faith is entrusting oneself to the infinite concern of the Unique who creates, liberates, and grants participation in eternal life. Whoever realizes what God's self-presentation means feels invited to trust and confidence: if God really is concerned about me, us, all humans, where else could i turn to succeed in living this life?

Of course, entrusting oneself to God includes basic "belief," but the particular tenets or "articles" of faith express and refer us back to a unified affective nucleus that has the character of a deep—the deepest—adherence to and sympathy with "whatever God reveals to me."

There are many reasons why we cannot invent what it means to be accepted as an interlocutor of God. If God is infinite (infinitely concerned, caring, lovable, loving, etc), all our (finite) predicates are infinitely inadequate, even the negative predicates we use to display the contradictions that refer to an "eminent," but still unknown, meaning that better suits God's essence.[9] Moreover, if it is true that being human is *essentially* God-related—if the fundamental definition of a human being is *animal orans*—then even our self-knowledge cannot be adequate, because our very relation to God (and therewith our own most defining being) is marked by God's blinding infinity. If only a non-objectifiable, mysterious, and engaged God is believable, being human itself also will remain a mysterious non-object. To what extent this still permits us to understand humans as subjects, we will ask further on.

Trust—Gratitude—Hope

As free concretization of the human essence, faith cannot comprehend itself; but we experience how faith unfolds in a constellation of dispositions, virtues, practices, beliefs, and, yes, also theologies and philosophies. With regard to the "content" of Christian faith we should not restrict it to that part or kind of truth that only can be revealed but never discovered by common sense or philosophically. If faith were sealed off from all "natural" truth, nobody could understand the earthly signs of God's surprising self-revelation. On the other hand, the partial truth of common sense and philosophy cannot show its full meaning without displaying its intimate links with the revealed aspects of God's presence in humans' worldly and historical life. The content of faith cannot be defined by adding "facts of faith" to the knowledge we acquire through common sense and philosophy. Such "facts," for example the contents of Jesus' preaching and the stories about his resurrection, can be read and studied through several disciplines without inducing any faith. "Religious studies" do not know what an encounter with God means, unless they also see all facts in the light and from the perspective of a faithful looking up that looks down on all study (without demeaning it).

In faith, God's "speaking" addresses me, who answer God in trust, gratitude, and hope. *Trust* is justified by the experience of having received everything, including faith, from God, who—I am convinced—cares for me, for us. It includes *gratitude* for the splendor of creation and history, even if the many scandalous forms of evil continue to outrage us. Faith also includes *hope*, because we are confident that the caring God will continue to create and liberate. Gratitude, trust, and hope belong together and overlap. They correspond to God's presence in his "Word," which accompanies us "yesterday, today, and onto eternity."[10] Thus, they open us toward the eternity of God's dialogical presence "in" and beyond time.

Faith itself does not speak in terms of finiteness and infinity, except when Christian philosophers and philosophically educated theologians reflect on it. This does not mean that we should not use these and other *philosophoumena* in our attempts at approaching God. Those who want to shield the Christian faith against all philosophical contamination seem to assume that other types of language and literary genre (everyday language, narrative, poetry, fable, myth, address, exegesis, and so on) are purer than the conceptual language of philosophy. What is their justification for this prejudice? Are narratives and poetry, for example, immune against idolatry? The philosophical distinctions between finitude and infinity and between the latter and totality are very helpful to prevent infantile, sentimental, empiricist, and rationalist modes of understanding that God is good, just, a rock, a father, a compassionate helper in misery, and so on.

Philosophy cannot submit faith to its own scope, but it is welcome to assist the ongoing self-purification through which faith remains a search for understanding the truth it already embraces but never fathoms adequately. The biggest mistake one can make in thinking about God is to absolutize any tool, image, concept, proposition, theory, language, genre, framework, or vision—thus erecting them as idols. However, all of them can be converted into elements of faith itself.

Converted from what? The faith of a Christian praises God as creator, but it also recognizes that we are impure and wounded by a history of disloyalty and arrogance. We are seduced by many attempts at playing God. Idolization and self-idolization, however strange and stupid, permeate our lives. We are worse than we can and should be, but we imagine ourselves on top of all things. Our history is a history of greed, violence, injustice, indifference, and cruelty. How can the Creator continue to love us, who are not only finite, but also disgusting in our mixture of arrogance and injustice?

Faith thanks for more than existence: although honesty demands us to say "i am not worthy," God is compassionate and forgiving. The encounter of human sin and divine forgiveness is summarized in the crucifixion of the utmost generous man Jesus, the Christ. His passion summarizes the coincidence of ongoing injustice committed by humans against other humans with the arrogant rejection of God's presence in history; but it also reveals God's loving and lovable humility. All violence, greed, and injustice of human history are judged and forgiven on the cross and transformed into the God-given peace of Jesus' resurrection. The holy story of utmost humiliation and highest elevation shows how the history of human virtue and sin is transfigured into a history of life-granting conversion and grace. Christian faith believes that the God of creation is the God of sanctification-despite-sin.

Since both creation and sanctification originate in God, they presuppose one another: we exist because God is gracious. The sources of Christianity summarize the history of religion by finding everywhere hints and traces, shadows, mirrorings, and prefigurations of God's indestructible love. All the prayers, rituals, and sacraments of the Christian religion express and realize this incredible, but true, originary, infinite, creative, and transforming love. Trust, gratitude, and hope are thus three aspects of one unified human response to the originary Love that provokes it. This response is perfect if it is the deepest and greatest love of which humans are capable: a love which, in its own mode, echoes the love of God.

Love

From the beginning of Christianity, its thinkers have been struck by similarities between the Platonists' descriptions of *erōs* and Christian *agapē*. Despite Anders Nygren's influential attempt to strongly contrast these two kinds of love,[11] it remains possible to recognize the differences between them without denying that they share important elements. If, from the perspective of Christian faith, Plato's hymns to *erōs* in the *Banquet* and the *Phaedrus* are fourth-century Athenian attempts to discover the originary drive that motivates all human individuals, we must recognize (1) that his philosophy of *erōs* has dominated entire continents of the European philosophical, literary, artistic, and theological culture; (2) that it is hardly possible to deny the erotic experience that inspired Plato's descriptions, even if we may debate his interpretations; and (3) that Christian or other faiths in salvation and beatitude would not be understandable if they did not respond to a more or less similar, fundamental and all-decisive, drive that inspires all human lives. The "spirit" of non-Christian Platonism is certainly different from that of Christian faith and any theology that comments on it, but even so, it does not exclude a conversion to the spirit of the gospel and its transformation into an element of Christian theology, as a constant long stream of contemplative and mystical literature has demonstrated.[12]

It is not necessary to study in detail how exactly Platonic philosophy and Christian thought relate to one another in order to use Platonic elements in an explanation of Christian love. Some critics have emphasized the danger that a Platonizing orientation in theology easily leads to a solipsistic intimacy of the soul with God. The framework that young Augustine, shortly after his conversion, set up for his dialogue with God, for example, seems to neglect all other individuals, when he declares: "I desire to know God and the soul . . . Nothing else." True, "the soul" may here represent all human souls, and his declaration is followed by the statement that he loves his friends; but it is not clear how other individuals participate in his soliloquy with God. Neither is it clear how his reflection fits into his friendships and into the prayerful address with which his *Soliloquium* begins.[13] Does his prayer continue in the background of his discussion? Does it play a role in making him wiser on the way to truth?

The faith of an authentic Christian does not tolerate any separation between love for God and love for all neighbors, as Bishop Augustine emphasized in his later treatise *On the Christian Doctrine.* Apparently he needed time to discover certain aspects of the faith he had already found but had not yet explored enough. Even in this later treatise he was not yet able to conceptualize the unbreakable unity between the two loves—or the two sides of one love—in which he clearly believed. He used the distinction between end and means that belongs to common sense and the average philosophy of his time, but he must also have felt that the subordination of neighborly love as means to another love degrades the neighbor by not emphasizing that love is false if it does not love the beloved for him- or herself.[14]

That Augustine presents his dialogue with himself as framed and supported by his prayer attests that he does not submit God to the tribunal of his investigative mind, but instead addresses himself and his concerns to the Incomparable, who dominates every possible tribunal. As a Christian philosopher, however, he would like to understand why God's concern for humanity goes so far that God's love declares itself identical with the love with which human creatures should love one another. God's philanthropy coincides with human *agape, caritas,* universal fraternity, brotherly and sisterly dedication, service, humility—embracing, achieving, enjoying, and enduring one's life as a life for others. How can God's infinite transcendence participate in a drama where humble benevolence is intermingled with world-historical robbery, destruction, slavery, murder, extermination, and genocide? How can the agapeic representation of the Infinite amidst the jubilant injustice of tyrants and empires reveal God and human destiny?

To be a Christian is to testify to the corporeal presence of God—through the spirit of his Word's incarnation—in this good-and-evil history. Unnoticed by world history, Jesus signifies the "assumption" of humankind into God's own life.

Over the years, the Church has developed a sophisticated theology of God's trinity, which transcends not only all totalities but also the entire space and time of humans who aspire toward the inscrutable God who allows them to address him. Transcendence surpasses the world by descending and emptying itself of its divinity.[15] If the "Word" (or "the Son") of "the Father" becomes human and dies to unite humanity with God, and if the Spirit, who unites the Son (or the Word) with the Father, breathes the new, divine life of Jesus' resurrection into the followers of his living and dying, then the trinitarian articulation of God-self is the horizonless "framework" within which the faithful—as created and redeemed in the Son and (re)animated by the Spirit—participate in God's life. Thus, Christians discover themselves to be inspired by the Spirit, with and "in" Christ, the human God, thanking and adoring the Origin, who is also the Completion. With regard to our loyalty to the world, this adoration means that faith in God realizes itself as devotion to the other participants of our history. If it is God's Word that humiliated itself by becoming a fragile, despised, suffering, and unjustly executed person, his spirit convinces us that we must continue a divine history of compassion and sacrifice for all.

The thinking of Christians who are also philosophers is part of one and the same ascending and descending love. Urged by the Spirit to focus on the weak and poor, they discover that their solidarity is a true form of adoration. In faith, the face of all humans appears as the face of Christ, who is the face of God. The spirit of Love is the breath of life. It enlightens prayer and invites a kind of contemplation that follows and prepares adoration. Reflection cannot objectify God's infinity, but can only annotate, comment from out of the margins, and laterally refer to well-focused prayers. Philosophy and theology find their right place when they, as footnotes to charitable devotion, are integrated into transdescendence.

A Faithful Life

If it is true that Jesus' agony was only the dark side of his undying life "at the right hand of the Father," the crucified God proclaims the truth of history. What do Christians learn from that murder? How can it summarize God's revelation about human history?

The crucifixion of this innocent man summarizes the oceans of injustice that in all times shatter innocent children, men, and women. The conspiracy of corrupt judges, honorless armies, cynical politicians, egotistical megalomaniacs, bureaucrats with imperial ambitions, and "decent" citizens who profit from colonial exploitation and political slavery continues to condemn, beat, torture, scatter, treat as garbage, kill, crucify, burn, and desecrate innumerable victims, and most of these vanish from the earth without leaving trace. All of us are victims, because we share in the debilitation perpetrated by the worldwide violence, greed, and selfishness with which we cooperate—Jesus' passion continues until the end of times[16]—but the weight of suffering is unevenly divided: while the weakest suffer most, the rich repress their shame and guilt with incessant entertainment and other drugs, while escalating their indulgence through more violence and contempt.

If all of us suffer, all of us are also the perpetrators of the massive injustice that since ages has infected the entire earth. However, Christ was crucified because he revealed the depth and height of God's human generosity, whereas we are not innocent, even if we are also victimized. The God who appeared in Jesus is too humble to please the corrupted smart and powerful, who behave like gods. In his crucifixion, Jesus shows that we, the crucifiers, sympathize with a realm of ongoing cruelty. Not only do we, the rich, enjoy the advantages of injustice on all levels of daily life, economy, politics, and culture; we also share in the hateful drives that kill benevolence and compassion. We live a comfortable life at the expense of the weak and poor.

While revealing how evil contempt and killing are, Jesus' passion also shows how God deals with them. The "natural" ties between crime and vengeance are broken, benevolence responds to hatred, patience to violence, pardon to cruelty, humility to arrogance, and peace to war. An entirely different realm begins here. The patience of a martyr does not eliminate the violence of injustice, but it displays the latter's self-degrading inhumanity, empties it of any justification, unmasks the jubilation of the winners, proves that their wealthy realm is a hell, and shows the possibility of conversion.

For all who think that "justice must be done—even if the world thereby perishes"[17]—it is a scandal that Jesus not only suffers patiently, but also forgives. Although he could pray that God smash his enemies, he forgives them and asks God to do the same, because they—the unjust who try to justify their acts through legal considerations—"are ignorant of what they are doing."[18] Indeed, the wisdom of pardoning endurance is a strange one for those who adore successful violence.

Among the gospels, it is John who proclaims with the greatest clarity that the death of this innocent man was, in fact, the enthronement of a new kind of majesty. On the cross, Jesus, the messiah, is inaugurated as lord of another, humble and foolish, realm, more effective in making peace, but also more hidden and more demanding than the guilty and unhappy realm where the strongest win. The mangled body of this faithful Jew is transfigured into the living sacrament of God's life- and light-giving presence in history.

Communion

Christian lives are animated by the spirit of Christ. Consequently, all Christians form one community, brought to life by that one Spirit, who shares God's life with the Word. The unity of Creation, Incarnation, Passion, Death, Resurrection, Ascension, and eternal Lordship—i.e., the life of Christ in world history—constitutes the sacramental paradigm of all Christian life. Inspired by the Spirit, as "adopted children" in the "uniquely born Child," Christians repeat, each in one's own mode, that paradigm by being citizens of two cities. While taking part in the material, natural, corporeal, economic, political, and cultural history as it goes, they know themselves at the same time participating in the trinitarian life that originates in God and embraces them as spirited speakers in the Word that continues to speak through them. The style of life that follows from this participation is described in the biblical sources that the Christian community interprets under the guidance of the Spirit. Obviously, the historical figuration of such a following needs to change with the political and cultural shifts of world history. Such changes are shifting attempts to live "in Christ," while at the same time being as loyal as possible to the earth, whose mixture of good and evil dominates the history of politics and culture. Thus, human history is one history in which several dynamisms are intermingled. As citizens of two realms, we share the humanized, damaged but saved, movement of God's eternity. The world is the still unclear and enigmatic cooperation of a self-driven history in search for freedom and happiness with a divine plan of divinization. What the world offers is a historical mix of virtue and vice, thought and stupidity, justice and violence, mutual support and hatred, while grace operates, mostly incognito, to convert injustice and corruption into peace and benevolence. The intertwining of good, evil, and grace shapes and situates each newborn person through education. We have become more or less well-adapted members of several histories which do not yet form harmonious syntheses. To live God's life historically implies a profound critique and reformation of the self-engrossed ethoses that mark the various epochs of world history. Each life struggles to obtain a personal balance for its participation in the history of good, evil, and grace. Saints illustrate how far the humble and humbling power of grace may go to purify all other drives, whereas the most terrifying of human monsters exemplify the abyss of hatred that threatens history from within.

Each life thus expresses one singular possibility of the Spirit's life-giving breath, even if this expression is always deficient. The intratrinitarian but earthly history that develops from Christian faith is unfolded (and disfigured) in all human emotions, passions, activities, professions, and monuments that are attempted. In all of them a typical combination of individual good and less good lives with the powers and "elements of the world"[19] expresses what the ongoing (re)creation of the earth—despite all its distortions—may reveal about God's union with humanity.

No epoch of human history is the only true or good one. All epochs have their own illustrious and debasing aspects. If we are wont to talk about "Christian" epochs, cultures, and histories, because of the influential role of the Christian religion in them, it is easy to show that they too lacked much in faithful continuation of Jesus' style of life. However, even in the darkest periods of history, it would be pusillanimous to think that God could abandon history to monsters alone.

Answering the Word

Have the theological considerations of the former sections distracted us from our central question? Don't these sections moreover exemplify the impossibility of speaking about God without subjecting the unthematizable to thematization?

The theological statements that were proposed seemed necessary to set the stage for a speaking that no longer thematizes but addresses itself to God, who "speaks" to us in various forms of revelation. But haven't we agreed that revelation and prayer refute all attempts to locate God within the limits of any stage or setting? However universal and encompassing a panorama may be, God does not fit into its horizon. God is adorable, "always greater" (*semper major*),[20] unfathomable, and incomparable, nothing like—and nothing of—"all that" (*ta panta, omnia*). Even the most radical kind of negative theology cannot conceptualize God, because (a) it cannot liberate itself completely from the positive theology from which it takes its departure, and (b) its negations continue to be said *about* God from the same thematizing perspective as any other theology.

As philosophers or theologians we are not able to overcome the typical perspective of the *theoretical* attitude, but trust, gratitude, hope, and love name another, more adequate relationship with God who addresses us through the signs and signals of a "speaking" that provokes our faith. Responding to the "Word" that affects us breaks through the horizon of the universe—without abandoning it. The whole (*to pan*) neither encompasses nor excludes God, nor *is* it the God, who is and is not in and outside the whole.[21]

And yet, we are not able to forget the created universe as a thematizable context from which we cannot and should not flee in order to reach out and ecstatically drown into a "supernatural," "backworldly," ethereal, or unearthly nothingness or being. Even when we adore God without distraction, we cannot stop being aware of the surrounding world and history, while imagining it as a spatio-temporal drama that situates us *coram Deo*. Our attention (listening, responding, devotion) to God, who is no part of our universe while permeating all of its details at all times, remains accompanied by a lateral awareness of the scene from which our adoration departs. We are immersed in the world, but we can focus on the One who offers it to us, while not being part of it, though being signified and hiddenly present in every one of its parts. Only this focusing—this responding to God's affecting and "speaking" or "appealing" presence—allows for an experiential reference that does justice to God's unthematizable, and in this sense incomparable, non-worldly, non-universal, and non-being unicity.

If the most radical definition of human beings is not "animal rationale" but "animal orans," such a response—listening and responding to the Unique's Word—is also the most radical mode of enacting the essence of the unique individual that you, in your way, are, or i, in my different way, am.

The dialogue between God and a human interlocutor enacts the "awakening," "calling," "listening," "responding," and dealing that connects the essence of the incomparable Unique with a multitude of unique i's whose essences are constituted and structured as living references to the One that does not depend on any universe, but through the *Logos* graciously participates in the drama of our human world. This dialogue—speaking in response to "Speaking"—occurs in human history. According to the Christian faith, it becomes a lie when it is sought as an ecstatic alibi for not participating in this history. Religious devotion without neighborly dedication cannot be authentic. You are as important as God. Our conversation is a test for the authenticity of our prayer. Not only does it express the graciousness that originates in the Origin of all words; it also can assemble the interlocutors in a communal celebration of that origin: a liturgical response in trust, adoration, gratitude, hope, and love.

Prayer and Theology

In chapter 3 we saw that *speaking about* you can and ought to be subordinated and integrated into a *speaking to* that does justice to your nonobjectifiable and unique selfhood. Speaking about God, including its theological versions, is even less adequate than the thematization of a finite person and infinitely more in need of a radical correction of any objectifying approach. This correction can be found in an attitude that we could call "responsive adoration" to indicate that our looking up and praying to (our *ad-orare*) begins as a response to some kind of initiative that is experienced as coming from elsewhere and urging us to respond.

Prayer and liturgy are as corporeal, social, worldly, and historical as all other human activities, but they point beyond all limits and reach, without capturing the Unique that transcends them. Between the narrative or poetic evocations of God's relations to humanity on the one hand, and the most sophisticated versions of negative and doubly or triply negative and "eminent"[22] theology on the other, there are many degrees of adjustment in speaking about the references that have been found in the "books" of nature and history,[23] but as long as all these versions are developed from the perspective of an all-encompassing overview, they are not yet involved in the liturgy that alone seems to be the most appropriate—but still inadequate—mode of opening up to the Infinite. If and insofar as adoration needs illuminating considerations of its own worldly and religious situatedness, theology and—as a theological condition—philosophy belong to the unity of prayer and thought that, for many centuries, has been called "contemplation." During those centuries, thinkers knew that theology (including philosophy) could not be authentic without maintaining intimacy with liturgical and private adoration, while also being aware that intellectuals can hardly pray without linking their prayer with anagogical and epilogical reflection.

The Universe (Cosmotheology)

From the Christian perspective the gift of creation is universal, and the universe can only be accepted, not refused. Acceptance presupposes a free distance between the receiver, the gift, and the giver. With regard to the universe, this distance, which seems to make rejection as possible as joyful reception, implies that the receivers are not simply included in the universe that is offered to them. If the Giver entrusts the universe to subjects who are able to freely accept it, they are—precisely in this respect—different from and not just parts of this universe, even if not only some of their aspects or parts, but also their very freedom and existence are included in the given universe. The given cosmos, our own givenness, and the relations between both demand interpretation to reveal what they—from beginning to end—signify about the pre- and transuniversal relationship between the giving giver and the given acceptance of the universe by the given receiver who freely accepts the universal gift.

Analogically similar to the offerings of the universe (or one of its fragments) through which human interlocutors propose their interpretations to one another, the dialogue begun by the first Word that provokes respondents is an incessant exchange of revealing proposals and grateful renderings. Affected by the Word, we cannot but answer, even if unwillingness interferes by deafening our ears or distorting the language of our mouths. We cannot stop talking about the universe, even when we speak to God or human interlocutors, but its radical givenness enables us to discover that neither God nor the freedom of our facing God and one another are integral parts of it. Neither universality nor totality can be the ultimate category. Even categoriality as such founders in face of the "speaking" (or "facing") that distances, from all totalities and syntheses, the fundamental dialogic that precedes, supports, and surpasses all onto-theo-logy because the speakers' responding to the Word's provocation surpasses and separates them from all integration.

Distance and Intimacy

If God, as creator, is completely independent, free, and gracious, and if you/i/we are created, but also "more" and other than parts of the (created) universe, the dialogue between God and us certainly remains mediated by our attachment to the universe insofar as it surrounds and concerns us as a world, but we are distinct and free and un-worldly enough to receive the world as a gift and—as mortals—to render it as a sacrifice.

The meaning of the world depends on the attitude in which it is received. Insofar as we are parts of it, various possibilities present themselves to our appreciation and adjustment, attachment or detachment. We try to make ourselves and others happy by seeking fortunate combinations of enjoyment and dedication. However, the originary distance between us and the worldly universe reveals to us that this whole falls short of what we originarily and ultimately are looking for. Apparently, we are reaching out to more, better, other than the totality—a "more" that cannot be satisfied by "more of the same." The universe of desirable "things" is ultimately and originarily disappointing, because we are driven by an *erōs* that surpasses all goods toward a beyond. This beyond delimits the universe without placing it into a wider, more universal horizon. While exposing the finitude of all that is by illuminating its essence, Desire opens the absolutely originary and ultimate perspective.[24] The discovery of this "perspective"—a perspective without horizon—is the first act of creation: "Let there be light!" (Gen. 1:3).

In this light we find orientation. It prevents all absolutization or infinitization by supporting the infinite distance that distinguishes the ultimate dialogue from our attachment to the world. Without this light, it is barely possible to avoid loving idols. "Distance" and "light" are here, of course, metaphors for the radical and irremediable difference between the universe and its beyond, between the totality of our desires and the originary Desire that testifies to their relativity.

However, "difference" and "distance" suggest too much separation. If we took these expressions too literally, we would forget that God is not only different, but also different from any kind of difference that can be found within the universe of different (and therefore finite) beings. As (infinitely) different from any (finite) difference is the Unique also different from any finite self-identity and therefore free for an intimacy with the universe that surpasses any other intimacy. In this sense, Saint Francis and many others experienced the originary and ultimate relationship as an incomparably intense union-in-difference beyond any love within the universe. The *"et"* of *"Deus meus et omnia,"* for example, remains unclear but very true insofar as it tries to express an experienced difference beyond the most extreme separation-and-union beyond all union-in-separation.

The dialogical intimacy with the One who transcends all universality is constantly threatened by explanations that construe another kind of world or universe beyond, behind, underneath, or above the world with which we are acquainted: a *"Hinterwelt,"* as Nietzsche called it, or a *"supernatural"* realm that we furnish with this-worldly but sublimized things and persons. One attempt of preventing such a dualism takes recourse to the word "in": God is and works *in* the world and in or *within* the interiority of persons. God is "in" all things and all things are "in" God. It is, however, obvious that "in" as well as "interiority" are as inadequate as all other spatial expressions to name the One who can neither be defined, nor described, nor named by any word, because all words fall short of evoking the Incomparable—unless they are transformed into pointers that refer to what they cannot name. To become such pointers, our words and thoughts must be made dynamic and energized: they must be understood as invitations, appeals, or imperatives that urge the hearers to follow a direction toward that which cannot be displayed by any concept or proper name. Religious metaphors refer by encouraging a good listener to participate in a well-oriented movement, despite their inability to show the moving orient itself. Whence does the movement toward the One beyond all beings emerge? When the originary Desire speaks, it instills a radical dynamism into our language: all words are then transformed into metaphors that transport the speaker and the sensitive listener by carrying them over the boundaries of the finite toward the unnamable that is meant and invoked, but neither seen nor felt nor comprehended.

If this "transportation" occurs, not only some sublime words but all words and all things—the entire universe—begin to indicate the beloved, who needs hiddenness to prevent all idolatry that would reduce his/her/its incomparable lovability to the desirability of special beings. If, in this clear-obscure, broken but referring outreach, the universe begins to gesture toward God, we might begin to understand why the medieval specialists of religion and theology called the universe a *book* and a *poem* in which we may read God's word, or even a *mirror* in which we can detect footsteps, traces, and images—however darkened and still enigmatic—of God's face.

If we were not driven by the Desire that transcends all desires, we could venerate only finite gods. The shift from a world with many gods or none to a world created by the one adorable God occurs when we discover the infinity of a deeper than deep attraction without name or image that prompts us to hope, despite the ultimate disappointment of "all things" (*omnia*). Nothing of "all that" is—in the end—"It": the absolute Desirable *par excellence* and *trans(des)cendence*. If this Desire is an illusion, a finite hope is still possible, but only in (1) a universe dominated by finite gods, or (2) a universe that coincides with "God," or (3) a God- and godless universe.

Faith and Dialogue

The distance that frees us from being caught, as a part, within the horizon of the universe's universality, liberates us from the ultimacy of rationality in its modern, universally valid, and logically necessary objectivity, without opening a freeway to subjectivism, relativism, or nihilism. The originary orientation for which the pre-universal and pre-voluntary Desire is responsible is very precise in directing us toward the Infinite, the Good, the One and Unique, God.

Platonic and Neoplatonist meditations about the relations that orient thinking and the universe to the wholly other but all-giving One have helped the long tradition of Jewish, Christian, and Muslim theology to forge words for the ultimate truths about the universe and its references to the One who escapes comprehension. Jewish, Christian, and Muslim mystics have experienced what theologians tried to clarify in "light" of that which grants us an originary and ultimate interpretation of the phenomenal and to a certain extent conceptualizable universe.

Are we talking here about faith? Not necessarily about Christian, Jewish, or Muslim faith. Insofar as the word "faith" can be used for a variety of basic and ultimate convictions (e.g., the fundamental belief of a convinced atheist, agnostic, or scientist), Plotinus and Proclus were certainly inspired by a kind of faith when they argued for the necessity of reducing the all-encompassing *kosmos noetos* of the spirit (*Nous*) to the One from which it emanated. Similarly, all thinkers who refuse to stop thinking until they can embrace a fundamental position with regard to the first and last things testify to a basic faith. Indeed, the "first" and "last" truth cannot be *demonstrated* with the logical means that are valid within the universe of finite thoughts and beings. Even Kant could not refer to God by other means than a *postulate* for whose formulation he took refuge in a combination of judicial metaphors.[25]

Faith, in the restricted sense of the three mentioned religions, is not, like Desire, an a priori and (ultra)transcendental drive or affirmation, but rather a free response to given existence, a position acquired or received (or both) with regard to the universe, as it is experienced by historically living and responsible humans. Desire, the a priori *erōs* or "*pathos*" that precedes and transcends universality, necessitates the emergence of a personal position, because no person can remain completely undecided with regard to the meaning or absurdity of "it all." From the standpoint of rationality-as-universality, any faith is a wager, but from its own perspective, once it has thoroughly attuned the person who lives it, faith confirms its own credibility. Those who allow themselves to be confined within the limits of the universe distrust the self-confirmation of religious faith, but what they might consider an illusion or a risky wager is experienced by the faithful as the right answer to their human Desire beyond desires and universal thoughts. If Desire were an illusion, the skeptics would be right: but it is not sure that their absolutization of finitude can be guaranteed without appeal to another basic faith. That faith needs to be granted and accepted, because it cannot be conquered and grasped at will, is certain, but how could it be accepted in joy without discovering how much it always already has been desired and hoped for?

However, so many people do not seem to desire union with God at all. Many ancient Greeks, for example, would deem such a desire incredibly arrogant, indecent, or a sign of bad taste. Indeed, however incredible and impossible such a union seems to be from the universalists' perspective of a closed universe, if Christians, Jews, and Muslims testify to the realization of that possibility in the form of absolute peace, they have been inspired by a tradition that comes from outside of philosophy. The universalist rationality of modern philosophy does not reach as far, but it needs and demands (or postulates) another beginning than its own, in order to discover—and thus to become free with regard to—the meaning of its confinement to universality. As soon as one understands the limitations of the universe, one cannot avoid asking "Why?" Agnosticism is humble insofar as it confesses its final ignorance. Another form of humility, however, is found in a faith that recognizes the "diffusive" gratuitousness of an infinite generosity beyond comprehension.

O God. . . .

NOTES

INTRODUCTION

1. By capitalizing Desire, I want to distinguish the fundamental and all-encompassing *erōs* that motivates human lives from the multitude of desires that Plato calls *epithumiai* and Kant calls *Neigungen* (inclinations). For an analysis of Desire, see A. Peperzak, *Elements of Ethics* (Palo Alto: Stanford University Press, 2004), pp. 73–88. As orientation toward truth, Desire originates and constitutes any philosophy that deserves existential interest.

CHAPTER I. I THINK

1. In this study, I use "modern" and "modernity" to typify certain tendencies that distinguish the philosophical mainstream from Hobbes and Descartes to Hegel, on the one hand, from premodern and postmodern (i.e., post-Hegelian) philosophy, on the other. Typifications easily sin by simplification, neglect of balancing features, and exaggerations. I can only hope that my picture of modernity is not too gross a caricature. In any case, it cannot be denied that, even during the modern period, many thinkers, such as Blaise Pascal (1623–1662), Johan Georg Hamann (1743–1819), Johann Gottfried Herder (1744–1803), Franz Xaver Benedikt von Baader (1765–1841), and Pierre Maine de Biran (1766–1824), have produced important philosophies that do not fit my description of modernity; in many respects, they are even opposed to what we are wont to see as the philosophical mainstream of their time. The expression "modern philosophy," as it is used here, thus indicates a tendency that is still alive, rather than the exact description of a historical period. Some of the sternest defenders of modernity live in our own time.

2. Cf. Descartes's split between theory and practice, which I take to be paradigmatic for modern philosophy. See the chapter "Life, Science, and Wisdom According to Descartes" in A. Peperzak, *The Quest for Meaning* (New York: Fordham University Press, 2003), pp. 123–48.

3. For getting acquainted with this critique and with the perspective and practice of phenomenology, I strongly recommend R. Sokolowski, *Introduction to Phenomenology* (Cambridge: Cambridge University Press, 2000).

4. That is, at the end of the eighteenth and the beginning of the nineteenth century.

5. This is expressed exemplarily in Kant's prizewinning article *Beantwortung der Frage: "Was ist Aufklärung?"* (Berlin, 1784).

6. For the culmination of the movement that runs from Descartes's to Hegel's conception of freedom as will that wills itself, see A. Peperzak, *Modern Freedom: Hegel's Legal, Moral, and Political Philosophy* (Boston: Kluwer, 2001), pp. 168–215. The next quote is taken from Descartes's paradigmatic formula of the purpose that motivates modern theory: "nous rendre comme maîtres et possesseurs de la nature" (*Discours de la méthode*, AT, VI, 62).

7. Cf. Aristotle, *Metaphysics* IV, 2 (1003a32) and VII, 2 (1028a10): "*to on legetai pollachōs*" (being is spoken of in many modes). As ontology, philosophy must sort out the various modes of the various beings' being and emerging, shining, surprising, saddening, enjoying, and so on, in order to bring them to language in appropriate ways of speaking. See Peperzak, *Elements of Ethics*, pp. 121–75.

8. It is not clear how, otherwise, we could avoid the arbitrariness of a pure subjectivism with its sequels relativism, skepticism, narcissism, and other kinds of violence.

9. For the allness—or totality—of all reality, see Kant, *Kritik der reinen Vernunft* B599 ff. (Akad. III, pp. 385 ff) and Hegel, *Philosophie der Religion* (*Werke*, ed. Suhrkamp, vol. 17, Frankfurt, 1969), pp. 393 and 429 ff.

10. Descartes, *Meditationes Metaphysicae*, Third Meditation, AT VII, 45–46; IX, 35–37.

11. *Soliloquia* I, 2, 7.

12. See note 6.

13. Any critique of modernity must, of course, begin by recognizing the masterful grandeur of modern thought and the lasting significance of those of its experiences and intuitions that we still can retrieve—despite our contestation of its absolutes.

14. In the course of this book I will give arguments for the unavoidable differences in thought that are due to descent, education, national and group culture, etc. Here, while describing the modern project, the question is asked to suggest that it creates a problem for those who swear by autonomous and universal reason alone.

15. Like the arts, thinking loses its vitality if it despises or ignores its originary traditions. All the renaissances of the West implied returns to the sources.

CHAPTER 2: SPEAKING

1. Cf. Aristotle, *Peri Hermeneias* VI, 17a25–27 and 19b5; *Prior Analytics* 49a6–7; *Posterior Analytics* 83a22, *Metaphysics* 1017a25, 1028b34–1029a5, 1045b29–31, and E. Tugendhat, *Ti kata tinos; eine Untersuchung zu Struktur und Ursprung aristotelischer Grundbegriffe* (Freiburg: Alber, 1958), pp. 20–23.

2. M. Heidegger, *Unterwegs zur Sprache* (Pfullingen: Neske, 1959), pp. 254–56.

3. My debt to Emmanuel Levinas, expressed in A. Peperzak, *To the Other: Introduction to the Philosophy of Emmanuel Levinas* (West Lafayette, IN: Purdue University Press, 1993) and A. Peperzak, *Beyond: The Philosophy of Emmanuel Levinas* (Evanston, IL: Northwestern University Press, 1997) is enormous, but the analyses I offer here concerning "the Other," "the third," and "my" experience of "myself" differ from his analyses on some important points. Cf. Peperzak, *Elements of Ethics*, pp. 124–41, 153–63, 183–85, and A. Peperzak, "Ethical Life," in *Research in Phenomenology* 33 (2003), pp. 151–53.

4. Cf. E. Levinas, *Autrement qu'être ou au-delà de l'essence* (The Hague: M. Nijhoff, 1974), pp. 47–49 and 54–61.

5. The question of whether we should focus on the author (a personal existence, life, the authorial voice) or on the text (textuality, intertextuality) seems to me ill-conceived, because we cannot even represent one without the other. However, the phenomenal relevance of each of the two moments is profoundly different (despite and thanks to their unbreakable unity). To reduce a philosophy to a mere text is to kill the author. Such a killing is a consequence of the egological approach described in Chapter One. Egology reduces all other thinkers to moments of my mastery, property, and showing off in thought.

6. About respondence and appropriation see also Peperzak, *Elements of Ethics*, pp. 98–101, 108–9, 119–20, 193–94.

7. Cf. Plato, *Banquet* 206c–209e and 212a.

8. I borrow here the expression *fidélité créatrice* from Gabriel Marcel, who introduced it (though in another context and meaning) in 1933. Cf. G. Marcel, *Le Monde cassé; suivi de Position et approches concrètes du mystère ontologique* (Paris: Desclée, 1933), p. 287.

9. Cf. Plato, *Banquet* 206e–209e on the mortal mode of participation in immortality.

10. On acceptance, cf. Peperzak, *Elements of Ethics*, pp. 42–44, 115–17, and 169–71.

11. M. Heidegger, *Sein und Zeit* §§ 25–27 and § 34.

12. Cf. E. Levinas, *Totalité et Infini* (The Hague: M. Nijhoff, 1961), pp. 3–10 and passim.

13. Aristotle, *Politics* I,2 (1253b1–1255b40); G. W. F. Hegel, *Phänomenologie des Geistes*, Gesammelte Werke (Hamburg, Meiner, 1980) 9: 109–116,. A. Kojève, *Introduction à la lecture de Hegel* (Paris: Gallimard, 1947).

14. In this study, "economy" has the very broad meaning of a network of significant references having its own coherence. It forms a kind of globality or open-ended totality.

CHAPTER 3. PHILOSOPHY AS CONVERSATION

1. See "La Référence érotique des négations théocentriques," in *Théologie Négative* ed. M. Olivetti (Padua: CEDAM, 2003), pp. 83–94. For the Neoplatonic background of this passage, cf. the splendid and illuminating introduction to Neoplatonism by K. Corrigan, *Reading Plotinus* (West Lafayette, IN: Purdue University Press, 2004), especially pp. 163–88 and 228–39.

2. Aristotle, *On the Soul* III, 8 (431b20–22).

3. Cf. Aristotle, *Nicomachean Ethics*, VIII, 3 (1156b7–32).

4. Cf. the Third Part of Descartes, *Discours de la méthode* (AT VI, p. 22ff) and Peperzak, "Life, Science, and Wisdom According to Descartes," in *The Quest for Meaning*, pp. 123–48.

5. One of the strangest—and irresponsible—things neglected in many American schools is the programmatic and professorial ignorance of the two thousand years of philosophical thought produced from the death of Aristotle to the epoch of Hobbes and Descartes.

6. On the relation between "natural" reason and faith, see A. Peperzak, *Reason in Faith* (New York, Paulist Press, 1999), and Peperzak, *The Quest for Meaning*.

7. Cf. Plato, *Politeia* 376e–403c.

8. Regarding the "godly lot" (or "share" or "destiny") that, according to Socrates, makes some people fit for philosophy, see, for example, Plato's *Apologia* 33c; *Meno* 99e; *Phaedrus* 230a and 244c.

9. "Act only according to that maxim through which you simultaneously can will that it become a universal law" (I. Kant, *Grundlegung zur Metaphysik der Sitten*, Ak IV, p. 421). The second main formula is: "Act in such a way that you treat the humanness in both your own person and any other's person always simultaneously as an end, never as a mere means."

10. Ibid., p. 435: as "end in itself," being human does not have a price or relative value, but instead an intrinsic value, i.e., dignity.

11. Cf. Hegel's logic of the concepts in *Logik* II (*Gesammelte Werke* (Hamburg: Meiner, 1981) 12: 31 ff.) and his *Grundlinien der Philosophie des Rechts*, §§ 1, 7, 32.

12. To emphasize the kind of equality in mutual dedication, which this chapter describes, I replace the English capitalization of the first-person pronoun with a more humble "i" in those places where that emphasis is particularly relevant.

13. Cf. the first of Zarathustra's addresses; *Also sprach Zarathustra*. Book I: *Von den drei Verwandlungen* (F. Nietzsche, *Sämtliche Werke* (Berlin: De Gruyter), 4:29–31.

14. If each you is "higher" than each me, you and i are at the same time equal and unequal, not only in relation to the other, but also with regard to oneself. The contradiction that seems to forbid this analysis reveals that your and my responsibility for one another and ourselves is transcended by a prior "dignity" that commands each of us.

15. Cf. Hegel's *Phenomenology of the Spirit* (*Gesammelte Werke*, vol. 9, pp. 103–18) on the discovery that the slave (e.g., Epictetus) and the emperor (e.g., Marcus Aurelius) are equal in freedom and rationality. The "we" that results from this discovery, however, does not change Hegel's monological perspective on the relations between the members of this "we."

16. Cf. Aristotle, *Nicomachean Ethics* VI, 8 (1142a26–30).

CHAPTER 4. FROM THINKING TO PRAYER

1. Cf., for example, Rom. 15:14; 1 Cor. 1:5; 2 Cor. 4:6 and 10:5; Eph. 3:19; 2 Pet. 3:18.

2. The early Christian theologians used the text of Exod. 12:35–36 about the "spoliation" of the Egyptians by the Israelites as a legitimation of their taking several *philosophoumena* over from the Hellenist thinkers.

3. See also "Philosophia" in Peperzak, *The Quest for Meaning*, pp. 7–22, Peperzak, *Reason in Faith*, especially pp. 89–129, and A. Peperzak, *Philosophy between Faith and Theology* (Notre Dame, IN: University of Notre Dame Press, 2005), chapter 6 and passim.

4. A. Peperzak, *Philosophy as Mediation between Faith and Culture* (forthcoming).

5. Although the greatest thinkers from Descartes to Hegel still confessed their faith in "God," the Jewish and Christian God was dying under the conceptual attacks of their handling.

6. See, however, L. Dupré, *Passage to Modernity* and his *Enlightenment and the Intellectual Foundations of Modern Culture* (New Haven, CT: Yale University Press, 2004); and M. Buckley, *The Origins of Modern Atheism* (New Haven, CT: Yale University Press, 1987).

7. Descartes, *Metaphysical Meditations*, AT VII, pp. 41–42 (French translation, revised by Descartes).

8. Cf. "Life, Science, and Wisdom According to Descartes," in Peperzak, *The Quest for Meaning*, pp. 123–48.

9. Cf. "La Référence érotique des négations théocentriques," in *Théologie Négative*, ed. Marco Olivetti (Padua: CEDAM, 2003), pp. 83–94.

10. As the Eastern liturgy says: "Christus heri, hodie et in aeternum."

11. Cf. A. Nygren, *Agape and Eros*, translated by P. S. Watson (London: SPCK, 1953).

12. Against Lutheran, late-nineteenth-century, and Heideggerian criticisms, a host of twentieth-century literature on the relations between Platonic and Christian thought from Clement of Alexandria to Nicholas of Cusa has shown how authentically Christian the integration of Platonic thoughts by the best early and medieval theologians was.

13. Augustine, *Soliloquium* I, 2.7 and I, 1.1–6.

14. Augustine, *De doctrina christiana* I, 22.20–29.30.

15. No Christian theology can be a theology of resurrection and glory without being at the same time and in the same thought a theology of *kenosis*, cross, and descendence. In a Christian context, transcendence and descendence, glory and com-passion, cannot be separated.

16. See Pascal: "Jésus sera en agonie jusqu' à la fin du monde . . ." in *Pensées*, ed. L. Brunschvicg (Paris: Hachette, n.d.), p. 575 n. 553, or *Oeuvres Complètes*, ed. L. Lafuma (Paris: Du Seuil, 1963), p. 620 n. 919.

17. According to the old dictum "Fiat justitia, pereat mundus," contradicted by the other one: "Summum ius summa injuria."

18. Luke 23:34.

19. Cf. Gal. 4:3, 9; Col. 2:8, 20.

162. Cf. the *Constitutiones* of the fourth Lateran's Council (1215), n. 2 (*Conciliorum Oecumenicorum Decreta* [Freiburg: Herder, 1962], p. 208): "quia inter creatorem et creaturam non potest tanta similitudo notari, quin inter eos maior sit dissimulitudo notanda" (because one cannot state any similarity between the creator and the creation so similar as not to be surpassed by a greater dissimilarity between them).

21. Cf. also Peperzak, *Philosophy between Faith and Theology*, pp. 180–94.

22. The *via eminentiae* is supposed to absorb and surpass both the *via positiva* and the *via negativa* of theology, but it is not able to understand their contradictory statements as components of a synthesis.

23. For the theological use of the book metaphor, see, for example, Bonaventura's *Breviloquium* II, 11, n. 2 and 12, n. 4 and his *Collationes in Hexaemeron* 12, nn. 14–17.

24. Phenomenological notes on Desire can be found in Peperzak, *Elements of Ethics*, pp. 73–97.

25. Aristotle would have been amazed when confronted with Kant's limitation of morality and politics to questions of retributive justice, especially on the ultimate level of religion in the *Dialectics* of the *Critique of Practical Reason*.

INDEX

acceptance, 46
addressee, 33–34
addressing, 25–28, 30–32, 40–44, 84–85, 107, 115–16; and talking about, 107; and thematizing, 96; modes of, 28; texts, 75
adoration, 142–44, 151, 155–57
affection, 31–32, 34, 36, 43
affectivity, 119
affinity, 70, 85, 92, 102
agapē, 148, 150; and *erōs*, 148
agnosticism, 163
all, 85–86
anamnesis, 89
Anselm of Canterbury, 125
appropriation, 31–32, 35, 40, 64, 66, 71
archē, 11
Aristotle, 47, 89, 132
asymmetry: chiastic, 50, 108, 113; mutual, 49–50
audience, 97–103; anonymous, 110
Aufhebung, 71
Augustinus, Aurelius, 125, 149
authorities, 20, 35–37
autonomy, 91, 135–36; as ideal, 63; in philosophy, 1–7, 10, 14–16, 21, 81, 137–39

being, 58–60; as nothing, 59, 142; meaning of, 59–60; universality of, 60
beings, 58–59
being-in-the-world, 32, 35–36

being-with, 46
beyond the universe, 159

categorical imperative, 94–95
catholicity, 131
causa sui, 2, 8
chiasm of asymmetry, 50, 108, 113
Christ, 128–29, 144, 147, 150–51, 153–54; in history, 153
Christian and philosopher, 136–37, 139, 150–51
Christianity: and philosophy, 136–37; and Plato, 148–49
cogito, 2–5, 9–13, 64, 68, 85, 90; and communication, 85; and humanity, 101–2; and the universe, 101; individual, 90–91; universal, 90
commentary, 117–18
commitment, 29, 75
common interest, 110–11
communication, 27, 32, 40, 51, 64, 85–86
community: nuclear, 46; of Christians, 153; of faith, 134–35; of philosophers, 18–23, 134–37; of speakers, 32
competition, 38
conscience, 52
contemplation, 125, 132, 157; and dialogue, 125; and philosophy, 132
context, 28
convergence and truth, 70, 124

173

conversation, 44–46, 50–54, 58, 71, 74, 87–90, 93, 97, 110–12, 114–15; and contemplation, 124–26; and democracy, 117; and dialogue, 52; and universality, 115–18; in philosophy, 71–72, 112, 115–17, 122–24
cooperation, 38
correspondence, 53
critique, 38
cross, 147; as revelation, 151–52
culture, 35–37, 40

dative, 26
death, 152
Descartes, René, 2–3, 8–12, 80, 142–43
Desire, 62, 68, 159–62; and desires, 161–62; and faith, 162; and universality, 162
desire for truth, 61, 70
destiny, 107–9, 110
dialogic, 158
dialogue, 13–16, 45–52, 54, 58, 87; and conversation, 52; and light, 159; and morality, 45–46; and sharing, 46; and system, 112–15; and teaching, 50; and unicity, 107–8; virtues of, 45–46; with God, 125; with gods, 125; with myself, 125; with you, 125
difference, 97, 159–60; and dialogue, 107; and distance, 159–61; and intimacy, 159–60; between Desire and desire, 159; between universe and light, 159; between you and me, 105, 108, 110; in union, 160
dignity, 95, 109
discussion, 87–90, 112, 115, 117
distance, 159–61
dogmatism, 112

earth, 153–54
economy, 47–49, 52, 68, 105–6, 109; of truth, 68
education, 34–35, 37, 40
Ego. *See* I *and* cogito
ego, 34–35, 62–63, 66–67, 90; and the universe, 96–97; and universality, 67; monologic, 24; phenomenal, 63; social, 95; thinking, 95; transcendental, 63–64, 69, 90
end in itself, 94

epigones, 66, 117–18
epistemology, 119
equality: in philosophy, 88–90; of you and me, 108–9; unequal, 50
erōs, 148, 159; and truth, 44
essence: and the Desirable, 70; and the Good, 67–69; and unique individuals, 69–70; beyond, 68
experience, 3

face, 47–51
face to face, 28, 49, 51, 53, 96, 110
facing, 51
faith, 92, 128–30, 140–48, 162–63; and adoration, 142–44; and belief, 129, 140, 162; and culture(s), 131; and Desire, 162; and dialogue, 161; and God, 140–48; and philosophy, 128–32, 136–37, 140, 145–46; and reason, 131–32; and theology, 130–31, 139–40; and truth, 145–47; Christian, 128–29; in God, 129; intentionality of, 140–42, 144; philosophical, 134; "preambles" of, 133
fecundity, 40, 44
fight, 47–48
finitude, 9
formation, 33, 35
Francis, Saint, 159
freedom, 8, 46, 48; and God, 137–39
Freud, Sigmund, 121
friendship in philosophy, 72, 86

given, 158
giving, 158
gnosis, 129
God, 8–9, 12, 128, 143; and demonstration, 162; and freedom, 137–39; and gods, 161; and philosophy, 126–29, 136–37, 143–44, 163; and the universe, 138, 141–42, 155–56, 158, 163; and universality, 163; and we, 158; belief in, 127; face of, 151; history of, 128; "in all things", 160; "in" the world, 160; infinity of, 141–42, 144–45; of faith, 143; of philosophy, 143; phenomenology of, 128; presence of, 146, 150; proofs of the existence of, 127–28; proximity of,

144; speaking about and to, 125–26, 143–44, 154–57; speaks, 125–26, 143–44, 146, 155–56; Spirit of, 150–51; transcendence of, 150; trinity of, 150; turning to, 142; union with, 153, 160, 163; word of, 125, 129, 144, 146; Word of, 150, 153–54
gods, 161
Good, the, 68; and beings, 68; and essences, 67–69; and unicity, 67, 69–70; and the universe, 67–69; and universality, 67, 69; in thinking, 72; love of, 72
grace, 147–48, 154; and nature, 133
gratitude, 38–39, 41, 146–47

haecceity, 91
Hegel, Georg Wilhelm Friedrich, 5, 8, 17, 19, 47, 65–66, 96, 128
Heidegger, Martin, 46, 59, 142
height, 47, 49
Heracleitus, 130
heritage, 40; Greek, 129–30
hermeneutics, 28–29, 53–55; and interlocution, 54–55
highness, 49, 108–9
history, 153–54
hope, 145–46
humanity, 3, 9; as *causa sui*, 2, 8
humanness, 156; definition of, 95, 145
humility, 163

I, 2–4, 7–13, 17, 22–24, 30, 49, 62, 75, 90, 93, 95; and rationality, 62; and truth, 62; as me, 105–9
idolatry, 147, 159
imitation, 38
individuality and universality, 95–96
inequality, 50
Infinite, the, 143, 159
infinity, 138–39, 146
influence, 34–35
initiation, 27, 83–84, 86–87; in philosophy, 78–82
injustice, 151–52
interlocutor, 30
interpretation, 39–40, 70
intimacy, 160; in dialogue, 160

Jesus, 129, 150–52, 154. *See also* Christ

Kant, Immanuel, 7–8, 94
killing, 47–48
kingdom, 152
knowledge: relative, 83–84; universal, 83
Kojève, Alexandre, 47

language, 25, 29; apophatic, 68; common, 110; first person, 74–75; particular, 104; universal, 104
learning, 37–44; time of, 84
Leibniz, Gottfried Wilhelm, 128
letter, 74–75, 110, 115–16
Levinas, Emmanuel, 46–49
life and philosophy, 60–61, 70
listening, 24–27, 30–32, 36–37, 41–44; in philosophy, 78–81
liturgy, 157
looking: down, 105; up, 105–8
lord, 48–50; and servant, 108–9
love: of God, 147–151; of neighbors, 149–151

martyr, 152
master, 49; and slave, 47–49
me: *See* I.
meditation, 125
metaphilosophy, xiv–xv, 7, 24, 91–92, 123; and wisdom, 121
metaphysics, 59
method, 72–73; and dialogue, 72
Mitsein, 46
Mitteilung, 46
monologue, 13–16, 93, 113; and dialogue, 90; and discussion, 113; and interlocution, 54–55; as dialogue, 125
mutuality, 49
mystics and theology, 161–62

narcissism, 97, 110–11
nature and grace, 133
Nicholas of Cusa, 132
Nietzsche, Friedrich Wilhelm, 160
nothing, 59, 142
Nygren, Anders, 148

One, 68
One, the, 160–62; beyond all beings, 160
ontology and anthropology, 59
ontotheology, 158
originality, 37–38, 86–87; in speaking, 58
orthodoxy in philosophy, 82–83
Other, 47, 49
otherness, 97
others, 12–13, 50–51

pardon, 152
Parmenides, 58, 60, 130
Pascal, Blaise, 143
passion, 151–52
passivity, 33
patience, 152
person, 94
personalization, 66, 70–71, 75
perspectivism, 91
phenomenology, 3; of thinking, xiii, 10
philosopher: and Christian, 129, 136–37, 139, 150–51; as hermit, 112; as interlocutor, 112; as respondent, 110–12; becoming a, 78–87
philosophers: and theology, 139; Catholic and non-Catholic, 133; Christian, 131–32; community of, 18–22; families of, 20–22
philosophia, 126, 129–31; *perennis*, 131
philosophies: competition between, 71–72; confrontation of, 71–72; individual, 71–72; unique, 71–72
philosophy, xiii–xv, 1, 118–21, 129–30; and affectivity, 119; and arrogance, 101; and authority, 20; and autonomy, 1–7, 10, 14–16, 21, 81, 137–39; and Christianity, 136–37; and democracy, 88–89; and desire, xiv–xv; and ethics, 61; and faith, 128–32, 136–37, 140, 145–46; and friendship, 72, 86; and God, 126–29, 136–37, 143–44, 163; and humility, 101; and individualism, 15–17; and languages, 21; and life, 60–61, 70; and *philosophia*, 129–31; and prayer, 126, 142–45, 157; and religion, xv, 1; and revelation, 131; and rigor, 119–20, 124; and science, 58; and solitude, 7–15, 111–12, 135; and speaking, xiv–xv, 78–87;
and theology, 126–35; and totality, 59, 65, 86, 158; and traditions, 20, 57; and transcendence, 151; and trust, 123; and truth, 61, 122; and unicity, 70, 105–8; and universality, 3–5, 7, 21, 131; and virtue, 119; and wisdom, 61, 70, 118–21, 131; as conversation, 71–72, 112, 115–17, 122–24; as history, 112–14; as monologue, 122; Christian, 131–32; community of, 18–23, 134–37; economy of, 56–57, 68; education in, 23–24; history of, 129–30; initiation to, 23; institutions of, 57; issues of, 58–60; leaders of, 57; modern, 1–18, 130; multiplicity in, 71; nationalism in, 21; orthodoxy in, 57, 82–83; pluralism of, xiv, 21, 83–87, 91–92; postmodern, 22; practice of, 23–24; professors of, 23; progress of, 16–17; singularization of, 64–66, 71; social, 12–13; teaching of, 23–24, 84–87; the republic of, 134–36; without God, 131–32; world of, 56–57. *See also* thinking
Plato, 44, 89, 93, 132, 148–49; and Christianity, 148–49
Plotinus, 162
pluralism, 42, 103; in philosophy, xiv, 21, 83–87, 91–92
polylogue, 51
poor, the, 151–52
praeambula fidei, 133
prayer, 142–45; and philosophy, 126; and reflection, 151, 157; and theology, 156–57; intentionality of, 144
presentation, 39–40
Proclus, 130, 162
prophet, 52–54
proposal, 111–13
proposition, 36–37, 42, 53
provocation, 30–31, 36, 43–44
proximity, 110; and distance, 103–4; and universality, 103
publishing, 115–16

rationalists, 121
rationality, 62
reader, 109–12, 115
reading, 24

reason, 62; and affectivity, 119–20; and faith, 131–32; autonomy of, 63; natural, 133; universality of, 18–19
reciprocity, 47
reflection: and God, 151; and prayer, 151, 157
relativism, 91, 122
religion, 129; and philosophy, xv, 1
religious studies, 146
respect, 105–8
responding, 30–37, 46, 110–11
response, 30–31, 33–34, 38; appropriate, 31
responsibility, 38, 44, 52–53
retrieval as creative fidelity, 44
role model, 38–39

said, 27, 29, 42–43; and saying, 39–40, 42
saying: about and to, 25–26; and individuality, 42
Scotus, John Duns, 132
selfhood, 46
servant, 48–49
sharing, 46, 50; thought, 64–66
silence, 112–13, 117
singularity, 115–16. *See also* unicity
situation, 86
skepticism, 122–23, 162–63
slave, 49
solitude, 30, 34, 48, 106; in philosophy, 7–15, 111–12
speaker: individuality of, 42; unicity of, 42–43
speakers: community of, 32
speaking, 13, 24, 25–55; about and to, 27–33, 41, 43, 58, 68, 107, 109–10; about and to God, 125–26, 143–44, 154–57; and categoriality, 158; and writing, 76–78, 85, 110–11; as call, 30–31, 43–44; in philosophy, xiv–xv, 78–87; phenomenology of, xiv, 29
Spirit, 17, 129, 153–54
struggle, 47–48
style, 35
suffering, 151–52
synthesis, 91
system, 13–14, 112–15, 122; and dialogue, 112–15

taste, 119
teacher, 37–41, 44; of humanity, 101
teaching, 23–24, 83–87, 100–101
temporality, 37, 40; interpersonal, 44; of teaching, 40
text, 28–30, 43, 75, 84–85; and interpretation, 39–40
textuality, 40, 78
theology, 129–30; and faith, 130–31, 139–40; and mystics, 161–62; and philosophers, 139; and philosophy, 126–35; and prayer, 156–57; and spirituality, 132; and transcendence, 151; eminent, 157; modern, 131–32; mystical, 132; negative, 155, 157; philosophical, 127–28
theory, 155; and truth, 122–24; and wisdom, 92
they, 50–52
thinker, 60; as unique, 65, 67, 69; Christian, 129, 136–37, 139, 150–51; individual, 63–67, 70; unicity of, 71
thinking, 63; about, 26; about God, 125–26; and Desire, 61–62; and living, 60–61; and prayer, 125; and universality, 71; as a right, 137–39; as dialogue, 91; conditions of, 72–73; freedom of, 137–39; history of, 64, 129–30; personalization of, 74; phenomenology of, xiii; privatization of, 64
Thomas Aquinas, 132
thought: economy of, 74; original, 74; personal, 64–65; shared, 64–65
totality, 59, 65, 86, 158; of beings, 60
towardness, 28
trace, 33
tradition, 33–37, 40, 44, 52–53, 118
transcendence, 161
treatise, 90–91
trust, 123; in God, 144–48
truth, 42–43, 62–63, 91–92, 114–17, 121–24, 130; and affection, 122; and convergence, 70, 124; and conversation, 122–24; and dialogue, 124; and *erōs*, 44; and history, 124; and multivocity, 67; and philosophy, 61, 122; and self-awareness, 122–23;

and system, 124; and theory, 122–24; and wisdom, 124; common, 122; existential, 61, 116; history of, 123; unique, 117; universal, 117; versions of, 44

undecidability, 29
unicity, 91; and universality, 105–9, 115–16; of her and him, 105–6; of the speaker, 43; of you and me, 105–9
universality, 42–43, 62, 68, 83–86, 96–97, 103, 158; addiction to, 106; and conversation, 115–18; and essence, 69; and God, 163; and proximity, 103–4; and unicity, 96, 105–9, 115–16; of philosophy, 21; of reason, 18–19; of the moral law, 95; of thought, 3–5, 7, 9, 13, 69; of you and me, 105
universe, the, 11–13, 32, 35–36, 43, 58–62, 68–69, 86, 108, 111–12, 157–61; and God, 138, 141–42, 155–56, 158, 163; and gods, 161; and human existence, 61; as given, 157–58; as world, 158–59; beyond, 159

violence, 47, 151–52
virtue, 39

we, 46
will, 8
wisdom, 92; and philosophy, 61, 70, 118–21, 131; and revelation, 131; and science, 120; and self-awareness, 120–21; and theory, 92; and truth, 124
Word, 156, 158
world, 32, 34–37, 48, 56, 111, 151–55, 158–60; and God, 161; and gods, 161; of philosophy, 56–57
worth and dignity, 95
writing, 24, 116; and speaking, 76–78, 85, 110–11. *See also* text

you, 46–47, 49, 75–76, 93–97, 105–9; and I, 46–47, 50, 74–76, 86, 93–95, 99, 105–13; and me, 51–53, 97; as instance, 94; as unique, 94, 96, 99; as universal, 96; for, 49

www.ingramcontent.com/pod-product-compliance
Lightning Source LLC
Chambersburg PA
CBHW031247290426
44109CB00012B/470